Contents

(Above) Hampton Court Palace, Middlesex, as it appeared in about 1555. On the left can be seen the Pond Garden, then the Privy Garden, with the Mount Garden by the river Thames in the foreground. To the right is the water gate giving entry to people arriving by river barge. The dome seen above the water gate is that of the Great Arbour. (Courtesy of the Ashmolean Museum.)

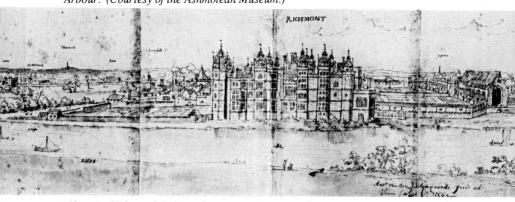

(Above) Richmond Palace, Surrey, by the river Thames, with an indication of the elaborate gardens shown in a drawing by A. van den Wyngaerde. (Courtesy of the Ashmolean Museum.)
(Below) The Great Garden of Whitehall Palace, London: a drawing of about 1555 from a viewpoint over the Thames, showing the garden on the left with a fountain in the centre. (Courtesy of the Ashmolean Museum.)

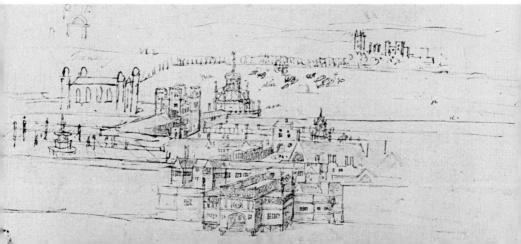

Early Tudor gardens

'Renaissance means rebirth — the rebirth of interest in classical antiquity which occurred in Italy at the end of the thirteenth century and was the dominant influence there until the early sixteenth century. It was in attitudes to man's pre-eminent place in the world that some of the most profound and pervasive changes in thought took place and they affected the design of the gardens and parks that surround man's habitations as well as the design of the dwellings themselves. From Italy the movement spread outwards through Europe, reaching Britain only during the sixteenth century. From then until well into the eighteenth century garden making followed a developing, but fairly settled form. The term 'formal garden' was not to be coined until the end of the nineteenth century but the use of formal geometrical shapes and the concept of the garden as a place where the hand of man was dominant rather than that of nature, were not displaced until new ideas of the garden as an idealisation of a natural landscape were developed in the eighteenth century. By then the inspiration of the Renaissance was, perhaps, rather faint, but the term 'Renaissance garden' may serve to describe the formal gardens which were swept away by the designers of the great age of the landscape garden.

Garden making is an activity of peaceful times when men and women may look forward to enjoying the results of their efforts. Thus during the middle ages, and especially during the Wars of the Roses, there was comparatively little activity in the making of gardens and such as there were seem, with some notable exceptions, to have been fairly modest.

With the coming of more settled times under Henry VII, from 1485, there was an opportunity for wealth to be accumulated, inevitably by a few rich men. After a period for consolidation this wealth began to be expended upon the conspicuous display of great houses set amidst equally great gardens. It was to be well into the sixteenth century before evidence of spending on these gardens became fully apparent. At the same time the amalgam of ideas we have come to know as the Renaissance began to sweep across Europe, affecting the way men thought of themselves in relation to God and His universe. These ideas included views about the relationship of the house to the garden.

Renaissance ideas of garden design were naturally overlaid on the medieval traditions of garden layout. Recent studies suggest that, while modest in extent, many medieval gardens were intended to be ornamental in character, even though most were mainly devoted to the growing of useful plants for food or medicine. Thus medieval secular gardens would have a number of walled or hedged enclosures with mounts, alleys and arbours. Many of these features lingered on and were incorporated into the new gardens, which thus became a mixture, sometimes well amalgamated, sometimes not, of essentially Renaissance features along with essentially medieval ones.

The first indications of what was to come were seen in the gardens of Richmond Palace, Surrey, built on the banks of the Thames up river from London as a symbol of the might of the new ruling House of Tudor. Little is known of these gardens save that they existed and were elaborate. Scarcely more is known of the gardens of York Place, Westminster, which was to become Whitehall, but of those of Hampton Court, Middlesex, as it was built by Cardinal Thomas Wolsey from 1515, we know a little more. Here there were turf-covered banks, raised beds and arbours formed of both foliage and painted wood. The impression is generally medieval, even if late medieval.

More evocative of the elaborate gardens that were to come were those of Thornbury Castle, Avon. Here Edward Stafford, third Duke of Buckingham, began in 1515 a very splendid garden around the courtyard layout of his new house. There were two main gardens surrounded by galleries of stone and timber and forming outdoor rooms with knots, one reserved for the Duke only. Beyond, there was an orchard designed for the pastime of taking walks in pleasant surroundings.

Hampton Court

The most spectacular gardens of the early Tudor period were those created for the King. In 1525, four years before the cardinal's disgrace, Henry VIII acquired Hampton Court from Wolsey and began a period of twenty years of building that at times amounted to an obsession. This elaboration of the royal palaces and gardens was but a part of a general elaboration of the court carried out for political reasons, partly perhaps in competition with Francis I of France. Another stimulus must have been the desire to set the seal on the triumph of the Tudor monarchy after the long dark age of the Wars of the Roses.

At Hampton Court Wolsey's palace was extended to make it fit for a monarch instead of an overmighty subject but it was the gardens that were the most distinctive feature of the great ensemble. Already heraldry had become a feature of garden decoration, and it was to grow in importance during the Tudor period. Wooden sculptures of heraldic beasts, emblematic of the King's dynastic descent, were set up in the Privy Orchard. They were painted in bright colours with much gilding and each beast was clutching a post surmounted by a vane painted in the Tudor colours of green and white.

From 1532 a series of three gardens was begun on the south side of the palace, stretching down to the Thames. These were the Privy Garden, the Mount Garden and the Pond Garden. The Privy Garden lay

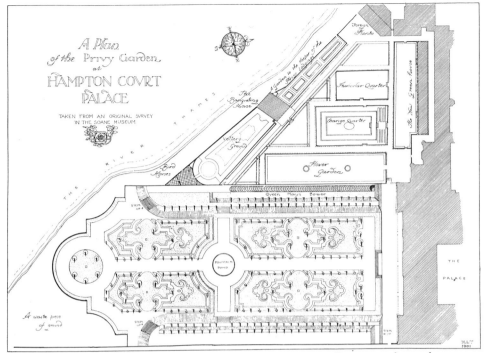

Hampton Court Palace, Middlesex: the Privy Garden and smaller rectangular gardens on the south side of the palace, replanted in 1924. (Drawing by H. Inigo Triggs.)

immediately below the rooms of the King and had two groups of square beds, each divided into quarters. Around these beds was a walk and to the east and west were galleries connecting the south side of the palace to the waterside by the Thames. Here there were more heraldic beasts and many yards of timber railings connecting them around the beds. There were 22 sundials scattered about the garden.

The Mount Garden was triangular and seems to have contained mainly apple trees but there was at least one beast. At the south-east corner was an earthen mount on top of which was the Great Round Arbour, a wooden structure three storeys in height, on top of which was a lead-covered cupola surmounted in turn by a beast and a gilded crown. This delight was reached by following paths through the quickset planting that covered the mount, attended by the inevitable king's beasts, this time carved in stone. From the arbour one had views across the Privy Garden and in the other direction over to the Thames, with the scores of boats on the river to be seen for much of the time.

To the west of the Privy Garden lay the Pond Garden. This had three rectangular fishponds laid out in line east-west surrounded by more king's beasts. Although doubtless used for the purpose suggested by their name, their use here in this form was mainly ornamental in intent.

To the north of the palace was a great orchard which contained another great arbour of several storeys. The whole vast layout was something quite new in English gardens. There was much that was French in inspiration but perhaps the outstanding characteristic was simply the scale of these gardens. The interconnecting galleries on several levels made clear the relationship of garden to palace and made it possible to look down on the various gardens and to appreciate fully the two-dimensional qualities of their design. Topiary was certainly a feature of these gardens at a later stage and probably played a prominent role from the beginning.

Whitehall

The palace of Whitehall began as York Place, the London residence of the Archbishops of York. After he became Archbishop in 1514, Wolsey carried out much building there, but in 1529 Henry VIII took possession and a programme of rapid expansion began, the rambling old house becoming the royal Palace of Whitehall. The result of all this rather piecemeal building was inevitably somewhat disorganised. There were even public rights of way through the palace.

There were certainly gardens at York Place under Wolsey but little knowledge of them has come down to us. By 1545 a large rectangular area to the west of the palace had been laid out as the Great Garden. This had brick walls on two sides and adjoined the palace on the other two. On the south side was the Orchard Gallery with the Stone Gallery above, whilst to the west was the Privy Gallery leading to the Privy Lodgings. Descriptions of the garden tell of carved columns with animals carved in wood set on top of them. There was a fountain, a new feature in the gardens of that period, and a sundial showing the time in many different ways. There were rectangular beds planted with low-growing herbs, surrounded by rails and with walks around them.

The gardens at Whitehall were thus very much in the manner of those at Hampton Court at the time, with the notable additions of the fountain and the great sundial. The inspiration must again have been French, and indeed there were a number of French gardeners in the royal service.

Nonsuch

The great palace of Nonsuch was intended by Henry VIII to eclipse even Hampton Court and Whitehall as a monument to his grandeur. Situated in Surrey between Ewell and Cheam, the palace was erected at great speed between 1538 and 1547, although it was unfinished at Henry's death. Little is known of the details of the gardens save that the

Privy Garden on the south side of the palace lay beneath the windows of the state apartments and that it was surrounded by a brick wall. A survey carried out a hundred years later reports on a squared layout with hedges. There was topiary at a later stage, although whether this survived from Henry VIII's time is not certain. To the east there was a knot garden and to the west a maze, presumably of the low-hedged type normal at the time and where one could see over the whole layout. Further out from the palace there was an orchard and a banqueting house set on a mount. This seems to have been an elaborate building with an upper storey with balconies and a roof ornamented with the king's beasts.

Thomas Platter has left us a description of the palace as it was in 1599. He remarks upon its situation which was so isolated that courtiers as well as visitors had to camp in a meadow from which the approach to the buildings of the palace was by a long avenue enclosed by timber palings. The name he reports as being most suitable 'for there is not its equal in England', and he writes of the wood in the garden, in the densest part of which many trees had been uprooted to provide alleys and vistas. Within the garden were a bowling green and a tennis court as well as a maze. In the pleasure gardens were imitation animals so artfully made as to make one mistake them for real ones. Paul Hentzner, writing of a visit during the previous year, 1598, remarks upon the extent of 'the parks full of deer, delicious gardens, groves ornamented with trellis work, cabinets of verdure and walks so embrowned by trees, that it seems to be a place pitched upon by Pleasure herself, to dwell in along with Health'.

Knots and allées

The outstanding feature of early Tudor gardens was undoubtedly the square knot, and it remained an important element of fashionable gardens throughout the Tudor period. This was to be seen in lesser gardens until the close of the seventeenth century, when the *parterre de broderie* had long been established higher up the social scale. A typical knot garden would comprise four square knots divided by paths and surrounded by a wall, hedge or *allée*. Knots had been known in late medieval times but it was with the great expansion of gardening ideas under the Tudors that they came into their own. Like so much else in the gardening of the period, the original idea seems to have come from France and, being essentially two-dimensional in effect, knots were ideally sited below the windows of the principal rooms of the house or palace so that the full effect could be appreciated from above. Gervase Markham, in his *The English Husbandman* of 1613, when knots were rapidly passing out of favour in the most polite gardens, defines two kinds of knots, the open and the closed. In the first type the pattern was set out in lines of rosemary, thyme, hyssop or similar plant, with the spaces between filled by coloured earths. Paths would be grass or sanded. Closed knots had the spaces between the lines of the pattern filled by flowers of a single colour.

No Tudor knots still exist and designs for them have survived only from very late Tudor times. Who designed them? There is slight evidence that designs for knots could be obtained from people who

(Left) An arbour and a knot garden from 'The Gardeners Labyrinth', 1660.

(Below) A garden with knots surrounded by rails and hedges, and showing watering and hedge laying in progress. From Hyll's 'Gardeners' Labyrinth', 1571.

Planting in progress in raised beds. From Hyll's 'Gardeners' Labyrinth', 1571.

undertook such work as a business along with designs for embroidery or marquetry. Undoubtedly many would be prepared by the owner of the garden or his wife and our evidence for the design of knots is largely derived from books illustrated with patterns intended to be adapted by garden makers.

Garden design in this period had not yet reached the degree of professionalisation it was to attain in later centuries and lesser gardens would be designed by the owner or his steward or surveyor. In the case of the royal palaces we know that the design and supervision of the whole project of building the palace and laying out the grounds was carried out by professionals appointed for that purpose. In the Office of Works the gardens and grounds were largely the responsibility of the Surveyor. John Needham occupied this post at the time when Henry VIII's palaces with their innovative gardens were being laid out and so it is perhaps to him that much of the credit for evolving a new style of English garden should go.

Early Tudor gardening

During the latter part of the reign of Henry VIII there seem to have occurred some of the earliest developments in the cultivation of plants in England. Religious persecution in continental Europe brought refugees to English shores. As well as textile workers who revolutionised English clothmaking, these refugees included gardeners, and their influence, especially in southern England and East Anglia, was of the greatest importance to the practice of English horticulture. The beginnings of the scientific study of botany can be dated to this period, for in 1548 William Turner published his *The names of herbs in Greek, Latin,*

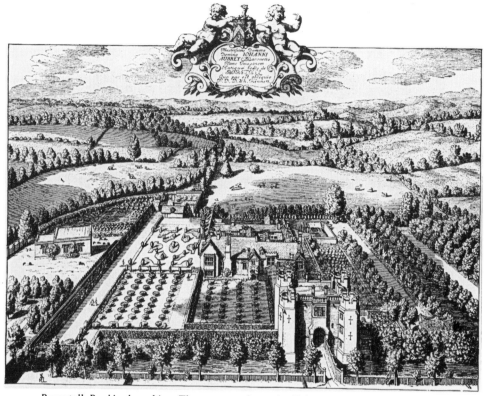

Boarstall, Buckinghamshire. The great gatehouse is all that remains of the fourteenth-century house, seen here in an engraving by M. Burghers of 1695. The layout of rectangular walled gardens and orchards is typical of lesser country houses of the time.

English, Dutch and French, with the common names that herbaries and apothecaries use. This constitutes the earliest mention of many foreign plants as growing in Britain and is thus usually accepted as the date by which they must have been introduced. Thus jasmine, paeony and southernwood make their appearance in the English literature of botany. Turner mentions certain plants as being found only in gardens and among these were the pomegranate, fig and almond. Perhaps as great an achievement was his great herbal published a few years before his death in 1568.

In this way English gardening reflected continental developments in the study of plants as well as in the design of gardens. It was at this time too that the earliest botanical gardens were being established in Italy, that at Padua being laid out in 1545. Whilst it was to be some years yet before botanical gardens on this scale were created in Britain, the foundations were being laid for such developments.

Elizabethan gardens

With the beginning of the long reign of Elizabeth I there was a noticeable change in the making of great gardens in that the initiative passed from the Crown to the leading nobles. The Queen herself largely made do with the palaces and gardens she inherited from her predecessors. Renaissance ideas continued to percolate from Italy but their passage was much disrupted by the religious wars of the times.

Elizabethan gardens have often seemed to subsequent generations to be especially evocative of the Elizabethan age and this is an indication of the important place garden making came to occupy in the arts of the time. The rose was the emblem of the Tudor dynasty and Elizabeth herself was often portrayed in the royalist imagery of the time as the eglantine rose. The rose appears in those portraits of her which were widely dispersed by her government as a principal feature of the cult of Elizabeth, the spring queen.

For all this we know surprisingly little about the generality of the gardens of the time, great or small. Of only five of the greatest have we even written descriptions, for no drawings have survived to indicate in any detail what these gardens looked like.

The greatest gardens were those created for houses designed to accommodate the court on the royal progresses. Such journeys to visit leading courtiers had been a feature of the lives of medieval kings but under Elizabeth they were seen as an important means of displaying the mystique of royalty. Besides accommodation for the Queen indoors, an essential outside feature of such great houses was the privy garden. This would be carefully distinguished from the more public areas. Normally the privy garden would be reserved for the noble owner and the public grounds would be intended mainly for displaying the social standing of the owner.

Kenilworth

We have a description written in 1575 of the garden laid out for Robert Dudley, Earl of Leicester, at Kenilworth in Warwickshire. Here the medieval castle was being adapted to make it fit for the times and a new garden was laid out just to the north of the castle. Occupying just over an acre (0.4 ha) within the outer bailey of the castle there was a terrace walk some 10 feet (3 metres) high from which to look down upon the knots decorated with obelisks. This was required because it was not possible to appreciate the knots from the castle. At the centre of the terrace walk was an aviary, probably of wood painted and gilded. The garden was square and divided into quarters by grass walks in the usual way. There was a marble fountain in the centre of the garden

Kenilworth Castle, Warwickshire: a reconstruction by Alan Sorrell of the castle as it might have appeared c.1575. The garden seen in the foreground was laid out as part of the restorations carried out by the Earl of Leicester and beyond can be seen part of the vast artificial lake which once almost surrounded the castle. (English Heritage.)

which was decorated with the Earl's badge of the bear with a ragged staff. In each of the four sections there was an obelisk surmounted by a porphyry orb and around it the ground was planted with fragrant herbs and with apple and plum trees.

Theobalds

Theobalds, the great house near Cheshunt in Hertfordshire of William Cecil, first Lord Burghley, was a courtyard house — indeed a series of courtyards. The apartments intended for the reception of the Queen were in the Fountain Court which was directly related to the elaborate garden layout. On the east side was the Privy Garden below the windows of the apartments of the owner and to the north was the Great Garden beneath the windows of the State Apartments. All this seems to date from the period 1575-85.

The Privy Garden was some 280 feet (85 metres) long and was enclosed by a wall within which were a gravel walk and a quickset hedge. On three sides there were rows of cherry trees and flights of steps that led down to a grass walk with another hedge and below this another gravel walk with a hedge 9 feet (2.7 metres) high around a square knot. The latter was planted with tulips, lilies and 'divers other sorts of flowers'. By contrast the Great Garden covered over 7 acres (2.8 ha), surrounded by a wall and divided into nine knots. Each knot was surrounded by a hedge of whitethorn and privet with cherry trees at the angles. The central knot had a white marble fountain and two others had flowers whilst the rest were grass, two with figures cut out in them. Later descriptions mention the approach through a loggia and a surrounding moat.

The inspiration for this enormous garden layout, much the largest of the time, is clearly French. Each of the knots had a symbolism related to the cult of Elizabeth as Queen. Its influence was immense.

Theobalds, Hertfordshire: a plan of the probable layout of the Privy Garden and the Great Garden. (Drawing by Ian Mackenzie-Kerr.)

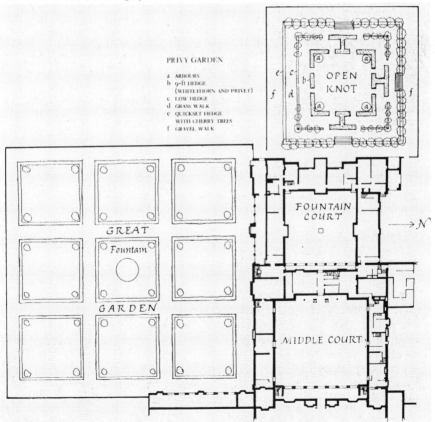

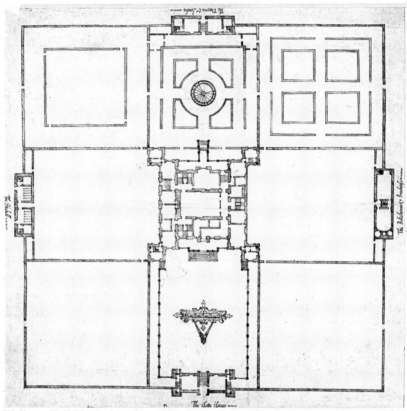

Wollaton Hall, Nottinghamshire. The plan by Robert Smythson shows the rectangular, four-square layout about the house with the entrance court on one side and a fountain garden on the other. (British Architectural Library, RIBA, London.)

Wollaton

Sir Francis Willoughby built Wollaton Hall on a hilltop near Nottingham, beginning in 1580, from designs by Robert Smythson. Although the extraordinary house survives, the original gardens have long since vanished. They were hardly less remarkable than the house. The layout was a series of rectangular gardens ranged symmetrically about the house with the principal gardens to the south. The centrepiece here was a fountain whilst on the north side was the entrance court. The side enclosures contained an orchard and presumably other kitchen gardens as well as the stable block. We do not know how this layout was constructed — whether the various enclosures were bounded by walls or hedges — but probably both were used. In many ways this was a

Aberdour Castle, Fife, where the terrace overlooking the garden, probably laid out in the 1570s, has distant views over the Firth of Forth.

Hampton Court Palace, Middlesex: the reconstructed Pond Garden looking towards the Banqueting House overlooking the Thames.

remarkably forward looking design, especially in the way importance was placed on a symmetrical arrangement of the component gardens, anticipating many of the developments that were to follow during the next century.

Wimbledon, London. This plan by Robert Smythson of about 1609 shows the original garden layout about the house, later extended with the large orchard and vineyard seen at the top of the plan. (British Architectural Library, RIBA, London.)

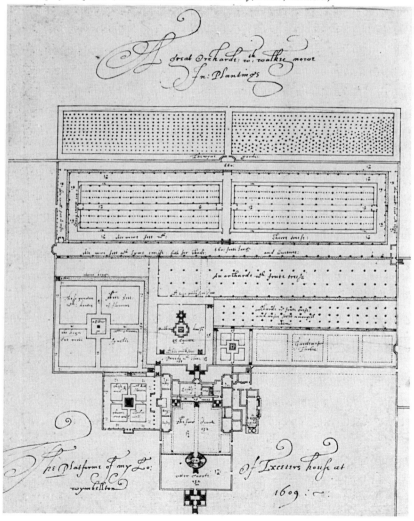

Wimbledon House

Wimbledon House was built by the eldest son of Lord Burghley, Thomas, Earl of Exeter. He chose a site a few miles south-west of London, like Wollaton on a hilltop. Both gardens and house have long since vanished and the main gardens appear to have been unremarkable with rectangular gardens set rather informally about the house. What was remarkable about the layout was the way in which the approach up to the main entrance was prefaced by a series of courtyards reached by flights of steps, the whole arranged in a symmetrical design which must have been most impressive. The inspiration of the unknown designer must have been Italian rather than French.

Nonsuch

The great palace of Henry VIII in Surrey had now passed into private hands and by 1579 was owned by John, Lord Lumley. He began considerable changes to the gardens which reflect his exclusion from public life because of his Roman Catholicism and his preoccupation with his ancestry. He had travelled in Italy and acquired a taste for sculpture, a rare taste in his time, and his alterations to his gardens at Nonsuch included extensive use of sculptural groups, columns and marble basins, as well as changing the heraldic commemorations of Henry VIII for his own. Throughout there was extensive use of allegory, in the Privy Garden based upon praise for Elizabeth I. The allegory became much more compelling in the less formal parts of the layout, for beyond the rectangular gardens were comparatively wild gardens. These were mainly groves of trees and shrubs with avenues forming vistas to open spaces around some architectural or sculptural feature such as the Grove of Diana. This appears to have been a basin with sculptural groups of Diana and her nymphs. There was a Temple of Diana, which was a banqueting house, an arch and a pyramid all designed with suitable allegorical associations. This sort of layout, derived from contemporary Mannerist designs Lumley must have seen in Italy, seems to have been the only one of its kind in Elizabethan England.

Other Elizabethan gardens

The fascination of the Elizabethans for allegory was carried to extreme lengths by Sir Thomas Tresham (1543-1605) in his remarkable building works in Northamptonshire. Sir Thomas remained faithful to Roman Catholicism in a time of religious turmoil and suffered harassment and imprisonment as a result, but he has left us the remarkable Triangular Lodge at Rushton and the garden at Lyveden. At the foot of a hillside was the Old Bield, a large manor house, and above this he laid

The garden of the Red Lodge museum, Bristol, contains this knot garden overlooked by the principal rooms of the house.

out a series of three rectangular gardens, the middle one being surrounded by a moat. A stone garden house, never completed, the New Bield, stood at the summit and from the cruciform wings of this structure one might look out over the surrounding countryside.

For the other great gardens of Elizabethan England we have even less record than these. The gardens of Holdenby, Northamptonshire, laid out around the great house built by Sir Christopher Hatton, survive only in the form of the earthworks of the terraces and two archways which once led into the base court, now standing forlornly in a field. This was, like Wollaton, a hilltop site and the house was approached through a series of courtyards. At Beddington, near Croydon, Surrey, Sir Francis Carew laid out splendid gardens around a fine new house and here he delighted in cultivating fruit trees. Many of his trees were imported from abroad and he is credited with having grown oranges in England, the plants being imported from Italy. All traces of these gardens have long since disappeared.

Gone too are the gardens, famous in their time, at Cobham Hall in Kent, where a tree was plashed to form an arbour and above that was a banqueting house. Just occasionally we get a painted glimpse of a garden in the background of a portrait group of the family but our knowledge of gardens of these times is fragmentary at best. The court of Elizabeth provided no central stimulus to the design of gardens or buildings and so the practice of design was dispersed and isolated. If there is a consistent theme throughout the gardens of the period, it is a preoccupation with intricate pattern, a feature of much design in other media at the time, and it was doubtless in the layout of the knots that Elizabethan people took greatest delight.

Scottish gardens

Gardening in Scotland, at any rate on a grand scale, had a hesitant beginning due to the unsettled political state of the country. James VI, before he departed to become James I of England, had an imposing garden beside his castle at Stirling. Perhaps its situation well outside the defences of the castle on the surrounding flat land was a demonstration that more settled times had arrived. The earthworks of the King's Knot,

An air view of the King's Knot, below Stirling Castle. The earthworks remain of the garden made for James VI and I, 1627-8. (Crown copyright/MOD; reproduced with the permission of the Controller of HMSO.)

with its geometric rectangular design, are still an impressive sight seen from the ramparts of the castle. No records survive of the planting of this garden but upon these earthworks there would have been fruit trees, shrubs, flowers and probably sculptural figures. At the centre there may well have been a garden building of some kind. The Queen, Anne of Denmark, had her own garden south of the palace but this seems to have been an enclosed one on more medieval lines than that of the king.

Small gardens

The small gardens of the period have left even fewer physical traces behind than the greater ones but we can derive some idea of the type of common small garden from written accounts. Foremost among these is that of Thomas Tusser (1515 to *c*.1580) in his *Hundred Good Points of Husbandry* of 1557. This gives a monthly rhymed calendar of work in the garden with lists of plants that were cultivated. The book went through twelve editions until it became the *Five Hundred Good Points of Husbandry* in 1573 and probably represents fairly accurately the accepted gardening practices of the time.

Such gardens would be quite small in extent, hedged or walled somewhat in the medieval manner. Dr John Hall wrote in 1563 of a garden:

> It hedged was with honeysuckles,
> Or periclimenum;
> Well mixed with small cornus trees,
> Sweet briar and ligustrum.

Elizabethan plants

Our knowledge of the state of developments in the cultivation of plants in the gardens of the period is inevitably drawn largely from such written accounts as have been left to us. Among these that of William Harrison (1534-93), Dean of Windsor, is probably among the more reliable. He writes of the increasing skill of gardeners in breeding improved strains of flowers with bigger and double blooms. There had been great improvements in orchards too, with plums, pears, apples and tree nuts of many kinds all much better grown than formerly. In the orchards of great houses almonds, apricots, peaches, figs and the cornelian cherry were to be found. Vegetable gardening had not been neglected and Harrison remarks that the cultivation of melons, cucumbers, radishes, carrots, turnips and many kinds of salad herbs had formerly been neglected but had lately come back into prominence.

Hedges were important but they seem usually to have been whitethorn or privet. Box and rosemary hedging was frequently used for the borders of beds but yew hedges were a later development, as was the widespread use of topiary.

Botanical developments

The thrusting, forward looking nature of Elizabethan society ensured that new developments and new plants were readily welcomed into the gardens of the newly built houses of the newly rich grandees of the age. There were, at this time, no botanists in England of the standing of some of those in continental Europe but the patronage given by enthusiastic and wealthy amateurs in England was to be of great significance for the future of English gardens.

A number of the foremost foreign botanists were attracted to work in England. Among these the Fleming Clusius, to give him the Latin name by which he was known in England (his real name was Charles de L'Écluse and he lived from 1526 to 1609), is perhaps the most important. His *Rariorum Historia* of 1601 was illustrated with wood engravings of plants and was among the foundation works of scientific botany. He corresponded with English gardeners and visited England in 1571 and 1581. He became director of the Dutch horticultural establishment and was responsible for the introduction of many of the bulbous plants for which the Dutch have ever since been famed.

Among the aristocratic patrons of horticulture Edward, eleventh Baron Zouche of Harringworth, was outstanding. He travelled on the continent of Europe and became concerned in the affairs of the Virginia Company. He had a famous garden at Hackney, London, and contemporaries marvelled at the strange plants brought there from the New World as well as from Asia Minor. He developed techniques of moving trees that were thirty or forty years old. As superintendent of this garden Matthias de l'Obel, a native of Lille, provided a link with continental developments in the garden, which became for a time the recognised centre of English horticulture.

De l'Obel (his name is remembered by *Lobelia*) was associated with John Gerard, whose *Catalogus arborum, fruticum ac plantarum tam indigenarum, quan exoticum, in horto Iohannis ciuis & Chirugi Londinensis nascentium* was published in 1596. This was in effect a catalogue of the plants growing in his garden and includes some 1030 plants. Many of these were recorded for the first time as being grown in England and the date of Gerard's catalogue is generally accepted as the date of their introduction. Gerard's *Herbal* of 1597 achieved even greater fame and was of immense significance to the future of English horticulture, but by this time doubts were being voiced about the reliability of his work. De l'Obel had written a preface to the *Catalogus* from which it had certainly derived a good deal of authority but it transpired that the *Herbal* was an unacknowledged translation and adaptation of a work by a Flemish botanist, Rembert Dodoens. The wood blocks from which the illustrations were printed were bought second-

The garden as depicted in Gerard's 'Herbal' of 1597. Although a pleasant picture of a garden of the times, the illustration cannot be a depiction of Gerard's actual garden as it is copied from an engraving of 1590 by A. Collaert.

hand and carelessly attached to the wrong text in many cases. For all that, Gerard's *Herbal* became the standard work for generations of English gardeners.

The most important plant introduction during Elizabethan times was that of the potato. The portrait of Gerard included in his *Herbal* shows him grasping a spray of the potato flower and the plant is included in the text. This is the first mention of the plant in any European publication. In view of the subsequent importance of the potato it is strange that the details of its introduction remain confused. Gerard states that he obtained his plants from Virginia. But the potato is a native of South America and was not grown in Virginia until a century later. The traditional belief that Sir Walter Raleigh brought the plant from Virginia is certainly untenable as he never visited Virginia, even if the potato had been growing there. The likeliest story is that Raleigh obtained plants from a Thomas Harriot, who had in turn acquired them from Sir Francis Drake, who had obtained them from raids on Cartagena or from captured Spanish ships.

Jacobean gardens

With the accession of James VI of Scotland as James I of England Britain moved decisively into a phase where royal patronage became central to all activities in the arts as in many other spheres. After the royal parsimony of the preceding reign prodigal expenditure resumed. The gardens of Henry VIII must have survived largely intact until the Civil War, as is shown by surveys of the confiscated palaces made under the Commonwealth. Many of the other great gardens of Tudor times must also have survived, perhaps modified a little as the repairs and replanting of normal maintenance took place. After the virtual isolation from continental influences of Elizabethan times there followed a period during which French and, through France, Italian influences became crucial. These influences can conveniently be summarised as the Mannerist garden and can be illustrated by the career of a single designer, Salomon de Caus.

Salomon de Caus

Of Huguenot descent, de Caus had visited Italy and absorbed there some of the literature of the Renaissance. He spent a period in the Low Countries, much of the time working on hydraulic engineering projects, before coming to England in 1608. In the service of the Queen, Anne of Denmark, he designed gardens at Greenwich and Somerset House, London. Later, in the service of Henry, Prince of Wales, he laid out gardens at Richmond, until the premature death of the prince in 1612 led de Caus to return to the Low Countries the following year. He had arrived in England with an established reputation as an expert in automata — statues and other sculptures which moved by the ingenious use of water under pressure. An interest in such garden features, a fascination singularly difficult to understand in the twentieth century, was among the outstanding features of the revival of interest in humanist thinking in Italy at the time. Thus the gardens made by de Caus in England were part of the Renaissance Mannerist body of European thought and among the earliest manifestations of Mannerism in Britain. Besides automata, there was an interest in grottoes (indeed, it was in the grotto that an ideal site would often be found for the choicest automata) and also fountains, terraces and highly embroidered parterres. The last were really a new form of the knots familiar from earlier times, but redesigned with more expansive, flowing lines to suit the new taste.

Somerset House

The garden designed by de Caus for the Queen at Somerset House, on the banks of the Thames in London, was carried out in the most elab-

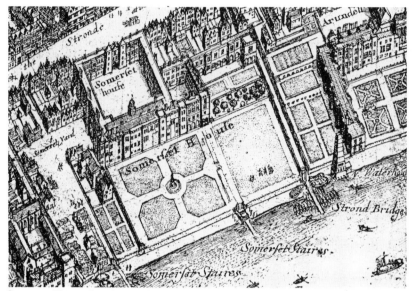

Somerset House, London, with its garden reaching down to the Thames, as shown in Wenceslaus Hollar's map of about 1658.

orate form of the new style of garden making introduced by de Caus. The garden was between the main façade of the house and the river and was thus a promenade where the Queen and courtiers might take the air by the waterside. There was a tree-lined walk down the centre of the garden leading to the water gate and steps where state barges would tie up. To the west was a garden surrounded by a raised walk, with a pattern set out by trees and walks. On the east side of the tree-lined walk was a circular layout containing an octagonal feature, a grotto-like fountain representing Mount Parnassus, with four river gods representing the principal rivers of the kingdom, and supplied by water pumped from the river. Here allegory came into play, with the rivers of England in constant homage to the Queen. Besides all these delights there was the more usual banqueting house and a building in which orange trees were kept during winter.

Greenwich

At Greenwich too de Caus was busy laying out gardens for the Queen but the work was mainly a restoration and redesign of the gardens of the old Tudor palace. Although we know very little of this garden, he seems to have combined small compartments into one and provided walks and parterres focused on a fountain in the form of a female figure pouring water out of a cornucopia and set within a basin. A further feature was an arcaded structure, a kind of grotto used as an aviary. The apertures at the sides and top were provided with gratings and there was a back wall decorated with rockwork and shells. Within were statues and fountains.

Richmond

Henry, Prince of Wales, had Richmond Palace as his residence for the three years he maintained his own household before his death in 1612. Whether de Caus played a determining role in the design of the new gardens for the old Tudor palace we do not know, for the Florentine architect Dei Servi was summoned to prepare designs for the work. We know little about the appearance of either buildings or gardens here but we do know they were very extensive and one of the wonders of the age. Perhaps the Italian made the Prince's architect, Inigo Jones, and his garden designer feel inferior for very shortly afterwards they both left for continental travels. Among the features described by amazed contemporaries was a great figure with rooms inside and a grotto in the base, and there were artificial islands. Throughout there was much emphasis on imagery, which calls to mind the imagery involved in the court masques devised by many of the same designers working for the same royal patrons.

Hatfield House

Apart from these royal commissions de Caus laid out gardens at Hatfield House in Hertfordshire for Robert Cecil, Earl of Salisbury. Cecil acquired the former royal palace of the Tudors at Hatfield in a complicated deal with James I whereby James took over the old Cecil house at Theobalds. Between 1607 and 1612 the new Hatfield House was built and its gardens laid out. The design of these gardens seems to have been evolved by a combination of Mountain Jennings, Robert Cecil's gardener, and Robert Bell, a London gardener who prepared the first drafts. This was then modified by Cecil himself in consultation with Thomas Chaundler. The latter seems to have been mainly concerned with the design of the East Garden, which lay beneath the windows of the private wing which accommodated the owner and his family. This took the form of a terrace near the house leading down to two gardens on descending levels connected by wooden steps and surrounded by painted wooden rails with a fountain between the two which drained into the river below. The fountain was in the form of a rock bearing a statue of Neptune. All this was got ready for a visit by the King in July 1611 but by the following November de Caus seems to have taken control of, at least, the East Garden. There were constant changes of design, with a new cistern to feed a new fountain in the lower garden, and in the two outer corners of the lower garden pavilions were built.

On the other side of the house the West Garden was connected to the remaining gardens of the Tudor building and here de Caus seems not to have been involved. Whether he was much concerned in the creation of the island and the dell below the East Garden is debatable as the island was part of the hydraulic system created by a Dutchman, Sturtevant. The dell was another island, although more elaborate than the other one, with formal walks radiating from a central pavilion built over a stream running through the centre of the island. Throughout these gardens there was a constant addition of new features to old and little evidence of any grand design carried triumphantly to execution. Yet these walled and terraced gardens descending the eminence on which the great house was sited constitute one of the great gardens of the English Renaissance and one which exerted great influence upon subsequent developments in garden design. Many a lesser garden was laid out on similar, if less extensive, lines, with terracing descending a slight hill on which the house was situated and with a faint echo of the Italian influences originally felt under the guidance of de Caus at Hatfield.

The planting of these gardens was undertaken by John Tradescant, whose fame was to eclipse that of all these people, for it was he who travelled to Holland, France and Flanders in search of seeds and rare plants for the Hatfield gardens. There were roses and other shrubs from Leiden, cherry trees, anemones, mulberries and redcurrants from Haarlem, besides bulbs, and more fruit trees and other plants from Paris. The vineyard consisted of a collection of vines presented by the wife of the French minister, Madame de la Broderie. The French queen supplied another five hundred fruit trees. Gifts of plants arrived from those who wished to curry favour with the King's first minister and Hatfield became one of the horticultural wonders of the age.

Garden mania

The Jacobean period was one of rapidly increasing interest in garden making among the wealthy aristocracy and gardens became larger as well as more frequent in the English countryside; indeed often they dwarfed the houses to which they were attached. Terracing around the garden became a favourite device, sometimes on all four sides, sometimes only on two or three sides, and the relationship of house to garden began to be more carefully designed, with the two being thought of as a single entity. The garden yet remained an enclosure walled off from the surrounding countryside where artificial devices might ape nature but must never be confused with works of nature. A desire to impress the observer with the monumental splendour of the whole composition becomes noticeable, a tendency that was to become much more apparent in the following century but was already making itself felt in Jacobean times.

Francis Bacon

One of the best known expressions of the ideal in Jacobean gardens is that set out by Francis Bacon (1561-1626), statesman and philosopher as well as essayist, in his much quoted essay *Of Gardens*. This is an evocation of the ideal princely garden rather than a description of any real garden. He begins with a plea that the garden should be planted so that there might be things of beauty to be seen all through the year, with enjoyment to be derived from colour and fragrance of flowers, the shiny leaves of evergreens in winter and the sight of fruits. Princely gardens should be of not less than 30 acres (12 ha) with three parts: a green entrance area of 4 acres (1.6 ha); a heath area, beyond the garden proper, of 6 acres (2.4 ha) with 4 acres (1.6 ha) either side; and the main garden in the midst, of 12 acres (4.9 ha).

Topiary and pools of stagnating water were not to be included, and Bacon had other dislikes:

> As for the making of knots or figures with divers coloured earths, that they may lie under the windows of the house on that side which the garden stands, they be but toys: you may see as good sights many times in tarts. The garden is best to be square; encompassed on all the four sides, with a stately arched hedge. The arches to be upon pillars of carpenter's work, of some ten foot high and six foot broad; and the spaces between of the same dimension with the breadth of the arch.

The whole essay is too long to quote in full but is included in many collections of English essays. It provides a valuable outline of the ideal garden as envisaged by one of the leading thinkers of the time but is oddly out of character with what we know of Bacon's own garden at Gorhambury in Hertfordshire.

Sir Henry Wotton

Another writer of the period who has left invaluable evidence of the gardens of Jacobean times is Sir Henry Wotton (1568-1639). In his *Elements of Architecture* of 1624 he gave his views on the design of gardens based upon much travel in France, Spain and Germany and conversation with the learned men of his day. After service as a diplomat in Venice he became Provost of Eton and was a frequent visitor to all the best houses and gardens. With his cosmopolitan background he must himself have considerably influenced the spread of Renaissance ideas about Britain.

Wotton gave his views on fountains: whether plain or ornate, 'all designs of this kind should be proper', meaning that where statues gush forth water this should be natural to the real figure depicted by the sculptor. He approved much of aviaries, which might have trees and bushes, running water and sometimes a heated room attached. Grottoes and other underground devices he considered to be 'of great expense and little dignity'.

Ham House

One of the best examples of these tendencies is the garden made by Sir Thomas Vavasour at Ham, Petersham, on the Thames near Richmond, Surrey. Both house and garden were built as new and were planned about a single axis which ran through the centre of the house and formed the centre line upon which the large central wilderness is designed. This has a series of concentric oval layouts of trees with walks and there are smaller rectangular flower gardens symmetrically

Ham House, Petersham, Surrey: one of the rectangular flower gardens either side of the house originally made by Sir Thomas Vavasour in the 1670s and replanted in 1975 by the National Trust.

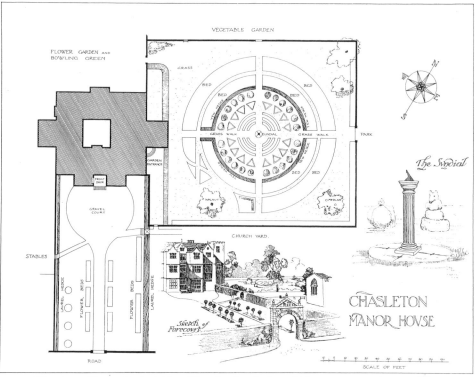

Chastleton House, Oxfordshire. The circular design within a square enclosure of the garden laid out shortly after 1614. (Drawing by H. Inigo Triggs.)

either side. There are raised terrace walks around the gardens and the observer could therefore admire the garden from two directions, either from the house or from the garden; in either case he might view a carefully designed visual experience that was intended to impress. This was new in English gardens and undoubtedly reflected contemporary French practice, possibly as manifested in the royal gardens being made at the time. An interest in the perspective effects of different types of garden layout is also apparent for the first time and this too was later to have immense importance in the development of the formal garden.

Chastleton and the Mannerist garden

One of the very few Mannerist gardens to have survived even partly to the present day is the garden made at Chastleton House, Oxfordshire, by Walter Jones, presumably just after finishing the house in 1614. The garden is placed to one side of the house and is almost square in shape. The circular layout of rose beds centred on a sundial and surrounded by a yew hedge has been likened to a diagram of the pre-Copernican

The Oxford Botanic Garden, founded in 1621 and the oldest botanic garden in Britain. The original layout of the garden is preserved along with the surrounding walls and gateways.

The reconstructed gardens at St Fagans, Cardiff, now the Welsh Folk Museum.

universe. Even though the garden was almost certainly replanted in the early nineteenth century, the layout is a fascinating reminder of the Mannerist gardens of Jacobean times that now survive almost solely in records on paper rather than as actual gardens.

Such Mannerist gardens were not solely based upon cosmological themes. The five senses might be the theme and several gardens are known to have been laid out as patterns based on the fortifications of the contemporary earth-bastioned fort.

The large-scale use of naturalistic water features such as lakes, islands, artificial rivers and cascades became increasingly important during Jacobean times. Often there would be a building such as a banqueting house or a gallery set upon an island in such a garden. Sometimes duck shooting seems to have been among the activities provided for, with tunnels of pleached trees along which the birds would be driven. Such features developed from the moats of medieval times which gradually became ornamental in function. The climax to all this came in 1628 when the strange Thomas Bushell began work on the grotto and water features at Enstone, Oxfordshire, that became known as the Enstone Marvels. There was a water curtain over the entrance and within water cascaded from artificial rocks and a fountain carried a silver ball on a single jet. Bushell lived in the rooms over the grotto but there was a hermit's cell and flower gardens with more pools at the foot of the hillside upon which all this was set. It was a fitting climax to a phase in garden design that was closely linked to the developing interest in experimental investigation that, in more serious vein, was to lead to the development of modern science.

Botanical gardens

This investigative and experimental attitude to the world had other consequences for gardens. The developing interest in the more or less scientific study of plants led, somewhat belatedly, to the establishment of the first botanic garden in Britain at Oxford in 1621. The first such garden in Europe had been the one at Padua, Italy, set up in 1545 and both gardens remain today very largely in their original form. Gardens at Breslau (now Wroclaw in Poland), Leiden (Holland), Heidelberg (Germany) and Montpellier (France) had already been established when Henry, Lord Danvers, Earl of Danby (1573-1644), provided most of the money for the University of Oxford to set up a botanical garden. The surrounding walls with their impressive archways and gates were designed by Nicholas Stone. He worked in the circle of designers associated with Inigo Jones and their Italianate form is, perhaps, appropriate to an institution that was also inspired by Italian example.

Lord Danby's younger brother, Sir John Danvers (1588-1655), was also active in garden making in the new manner of the age.

Greater Jacobean gardens

The tendency throughout the Jacobean period in the greater gardens was for the intricacies of the Tudor garden to be superseded by a somewhat simpler style of design. Although much formality remained, the characteristics of the site received more attention and care was taken to allow any attractive views over surrounding country to be appreciated from within the garden. Increasing Italian influence led to classical allusions being frequently included. A classical influence on design was important in inducing designers to grasp the significance of the garden as a whole rather than as the collection of somewhat disparate parts that had been the Tudor garden.

Lawson and the Jacobean garden

For evidence of the gardening activities of the gentry and more common people we have to turn again to the literature produced for them. William Lawson's *A New Orchard and Garden* appeared in 1618 alongside his *The Country Housewife's Garden* and the two were often bound together. For most of the seventeenth century these were the mainstay of advice as to how to plan and manage a garden. Whilst Lawson thought that the orchard should be the man's province, with the woman having the flower garden and kitchen gardens as her preserve, he advised that there should be no sharp distinction between them. Flowers might well be grown among the vegetables, although he recognised the problem caused by having to remove vegetables, especially root vegetables, to the kitchen, and he advised that such vegetables be kept apart so that the appearance of the garden was not impaired. Thus cabbages, onions, turnips, parsnips, carrots, saffron and skirrets were all allocated separate plots.

Among the rather strange ideas put forward by Lawson was that the layout of an orchard might incorporate knots and might have mounts at the corners. A maze, a bowling alley or archery butts might be added. If a suitable stream was available, a conduit might be arranged so that one might go fishing whilst sitting on one's mount. Fencing around the garden was given much attention and Lawson's favoured method was by means of a thorn hedge alongside a moat or dry ditch. A moat could be combined with fishponds or the conduit around the orchard. Where sloping ground presented problems, Lawson favoured a double ditch with the earth being thrown up between the two to make a raised walk and with evergreens planted on the outer side of the bank.

This advice was immensely influential in the design and planting of innumerable gardens of modest dimensions all over Great Britain. Most of them have long since disappeared but traces of a great many remain, perhaps just in the form of earthworks in a field, as fishponds, or perhaps incorporated into later garden layouts.

John Parkinson

John Parkinson (1567-1650) became apothecary to James I and had a famous garden in Long Acre, London. After the death of Matthias de l'Obel he obtained his notes and records. The principal source of information on plants that might be grown in a Jacobean garden was his *Paradisi in Sole Paradisus Terrestris* published in 1629. It contained details of about one thousand plants, most of them illustrated by reasonably accurate illustrations. The standard of observation was a great improvement upon that of Gerard and Lawson. He exhibited a delight in the appearance of flowers without the rather apologetic asides of Lawson, who seems to have thought that any plant not eatable or otherwise useful needed special justification for a place in the garden. Many acknowledgements were made to other gardeners and outstanding among these was the name of John Tradescant.

The Tradescants

John Tradescant first appeared in the records as being married in 1607, when, as we have seen, he was working for Robert Cecil, Earl of Salisbury, and travelling in his service in search of plants for the gardens at Hatfield. After Salisbury's death he became involved in the trade with Virginia, importing many plants, among them the spiderwort, later named *Tradescantia virginiana* in his honour. In 1618 he travelled to Russia attached to a mission led by Sir Dudley Digges and brought back both plants and notes on the flora of that country which constituted the earliest such information known in the west. In 1620 he was off to the Algerian coast, officially in pursuit of pirates but also looking for plants, among his treasures being *Gladiolus byzantinus*, the corn flag of Constantinople, which he found growing by the acre there.

By 1625 he was gardener to the king's favourite, the Duke of Buckingham, and was doubtless responsible for instructions to the Admiralty that ships returning from foreign parts should bring back plants for the collections of the Duke. Following the assassination of Buckingham in 1629 Tradescant became gardener to Charles I and began to collect plants and 'curiosities' at his house in Lambeth, London. Tradescant thus became one of the first declared plant collectors, for besides his own collecting he sought plants from various sources in Holland, from France and from Constantinople. Later he specialised in collecting fruit trees and in his list of plants growing in his garden in 1634 he lists 57

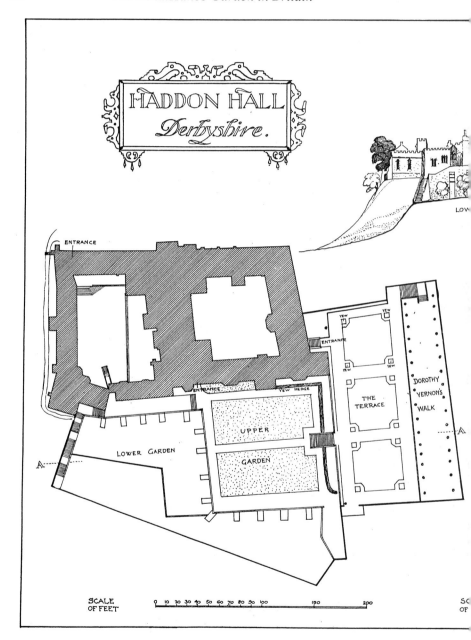

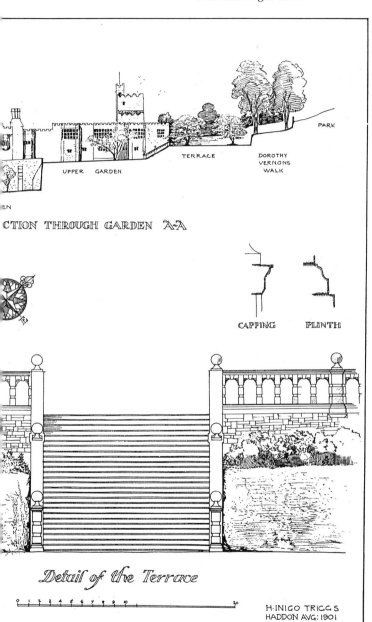

UPPER GARDEN

TERRACE

DOROTHY VERNONS WALK

PARK

CTION THROUGH GARDEN A·A

CAPPING   PLINTH

Detail of the Terrace

H·INIGO TRIGGS
HADDON AVG: 1901

Haddon Hall, Derbyshire. The drawing shows the layout before extensive restoration during the 1920s. The relationship of the layout to the steeply sloping site is notable (Drawing by H. Inigo Triggs.)

plums, 49 apples, 49 pears, 2 quinces, 24 cherries, 8 apricots, 9 nectarines and 10 vines.

William Coys and the gentleman gardeners

William Coys (1560-1627) had a garden at North Ockendon, Essex, where, in 1604, he first had the yucca (*Yucca gloriosa*) flower in England. Lists of the plants growing in his garden in 1616 and 1617 reveal strong North and South American connections for he had the choke cherry (*Prunus virginiana*) and the persimmon (*Diospyros virginiana*) besides both the common and sweet potato. His collection of Spanish plants included the ivy-leaved toadflax (*Cymbalaria muralis*), from which, it is said, that plant was to spread on walls all over Britain. Coys was a gentleman gardener and botanist and as such was the forerunner of a familiar type throughout the following centuries.

John Goodyer (1592-1664) was perhaps more distinguished as a naturalist than as a gardener but in his Hampshire gardens at Droxford and Petersfield he cultivated many of the rarities of the day. He was a great friend of Coys, from whom he obtained many plants, and he had seeds from Parkinson. He too seems to have had transatlantic connections and he was the first botanist to study the elm and to show that yews carry their berries on different trees from those that produce pollen. In 1617 he distributed tubers of the Jerusalem artichoke (*Helianthus tuberosus*), having 'received two small roots thereof from Master Franqueville of London no bigger than hen's eggs, the one I planted, the other I gave to a friend. Mine brought me a peck of roots, wherewith I stored Hampshire.' There were two Franquevilles, father and son, who were both London merchants. The father was a refugee from Cambrai and it was presumably from his connections that the artichoke was obtained.

Coys and Goodyer must stand for many other gentlemen gardeners of whom we know little more than their names. In London there were John Millen of Old Street, Ralph Tuggy of Westminster, Hugh Morgan of Coleman Street and Henry Banbury of Tothill Street. In Yorkshire Richard Shanne of Methley drew up a long list of his plants in 1615 and in Wales Sir John Salusbury produced lists of plants in his garden at Lleweni, Clwyd, in 1596, 1607 and 1608.

Little similar information is available from Scottish gardeners during this period. Although elaborate houses were already being built near Edinburgh and Glasgow, the gardens attached to the houses seem to have been little more than courtyards with banqueting houses and arbours treated in a purely architectural fashion.

Caroline gardens

The accession of Charles I in 1625 was as significant an event in the history of garden making as it was in very many other fields of the arts. The new king was greatly interested in such matters, although he had comparatively little opportunity for creating royal gardens. A great change from the virtual isolation of England from continental Europe during Tudor times was the opening up of France to Englishmen once more. During the reign of Charles I travel by Englishmen to France became much more common, and travel to Italy, the seat of Renaissance ideas, became possible. Whilst it was French influence that was paramount in Britain, the rather different influences emanating from Italy became increasingly important.

Isaac de Caus

As in the earlier reign, one man was to dominate garden design during the time of Charles I and this was Isaac de Caus, the younger brother of Salomon de Caus. One of his few surviving works is the grotto he made, before 1627, at Woburn Abbey, Bedfordshire, for Lucy Harrington, Countess of Bedford. This is an integral part of the house, a basement grotto, and so not strictly part of the garden, but it remains as a rare specimen of the Mannerist influence on garden structures. The roof is vaulted and lined with shells, and the walls are decorated with shells and rockwork. De Caus had earlier worked on the family London residence, Bedford House, and he may have done other work for the remarkable Countess. At Moor Park, Hertfordshire, she was responsible for the creation of one of the outstanding gardens of the century — all, alas, now gone. This had a parterre with statues, terraces, an area of fruit trees with walks beneath and a grotto. De Caus was particularly esteemed for his grottoes and he may well have created far more than can be certainly attributed to him.

Wilton

The work of de Caus for which we have the most extensive documentation is the garden he created at Wilton, Wiltshire, for Philip Herbert, fourth Earl of Pembroke. Although it too has virtually all disappeared we know a great deal about how it looked because of the plans and views made during its comparatively brief existence before becoming a victim of 'Capability' Brown during the following century. The fame of Wilton was that of the first truly Italianate garden to be made in England. As we have seen, this fame was, at best, only partially justified for several essays in this genre had been made but Wilton was the earliest manifestation in England of the full Italian Renaissance garden.

Wilton House, Wiltshire. The great garden laid out by Isaac de Caus during the 1630s. (Courtesy of the Provost and Wardens of Worcester College, Oxford.)

Moreover it was of the Venetian school of Italian garden design for, like the Venetian villas, it lies on a more or less level site and there was little scope for that favourite feature of Roman and Florentine gardens, the terrace. Wilton was essentially two-dimensional, a garden perhaps best seen from above as in the famous depiction illustrated on this page. Before the main façade of the house was a *parterre de broderie* of clipped box divided into four quarters, each with fountains around statues carved by Nicholas Stone. Beyond lay the Wilderness, a formal layout of trees with walks beneath whose shade the meandering course of the river Nadder cut across the formal pattern. Curiously the design ignored this unfortunate intrusion and simply bridged the walks across the river. The fact that the Wilderness was sited here was itself probably an attempt to play down the discordant feature as it must have been largely concealed among the trees and noticeable only from our vantage point in the engraving, from above. Beyond the Wilderness were two pools, each with columns, from the top of which water spurted from crowns which turned under water pressure. The outermost section was oval in shape, with a statue of a gladiator in the centre of the layout of cherry trees.

The whole garden was surrounded by a raised, balustraded walk incorporating, at the point where the centre line from the house met the raised walk, a splendid grotto. Visitors record enraptured descriptions of the hydraulic wonders within: figures wept water and there were secret jets which could be turned on to wet visitors if their enthusiasm should threaten to get out of hand. Besides all these wonders there was a water parterre and an amphitheatre set in the moderate hillside opposite the south front of the house.

De Caus returned to France, where he died, in 1648 but some years before that the Civil War had broken out and such civilised activities as garden making ceased. That so much is known about his vanished garden at Wilton is due to his having produced a book on the garden, besides a treatise on waterworks for gardens. His ideas were to reach their greatest influence after the Restoration in 1660.

The museum garden

One of the most distinctive of the types of garden evolved during the Italian Renaissance was that of the museum garden: a courtyard designed for the display of a collection of classical sculpture. The inspiration came from the court of the Belvedere Palace in the Vatican and scope for emulating such a collection of sculpture was obviously limited in England. The outstanding example was that of Arundel House in London, created by Thomas Howard, Earl of Arundel, following his return from his Italian travels in 1614. The Earl employed Inigo Jones to remodel the old Tudor house to accommodate the great sculpture collection both indoors and out. By the 1630s visitors were writing ecstatic accounts of the wonders of this Italian villa transported to the banks of the Thames, in spite of the problems of adapting a Tudor building to its Italianate role. The terracing alongside the river was decorated with sculptured figures, possibly the earliest Italianate terracing to be constructed in England. There seems to have been some effort to relate building to garden in a meaningful way and a suitably monumental atmosphere was created which was then quite new in England.

Gardens of Sir John Danvers

Whilst Arundel House was among the first of the Italianate gardens to be made in England, it was the garden made by Arundel's relative Sir John Danvers (1588-1655) at Chelsea that seems to have been the very first. John Aubrey wrote: 'Twas Sir John Danvers of Chelsea who first taught us the way of Italian gardens.' He goes on to describe the brick pavilions in each corner and 'fir and pine trees, shumacs, and the quarters all filled with some rare plant or other. The long gravel walks surrounding it were bordered with hyssop and several sorts of thyme.

Packwood House, Warwickshire: the early seventeenth-century raised walk around the main garden.

Edzell Castle, Tayside: the elaborately decorated garden walls.

Moseley Old Hall, Staffordshire. The parterre was laid out in 1963 but based upon a design of 1640.

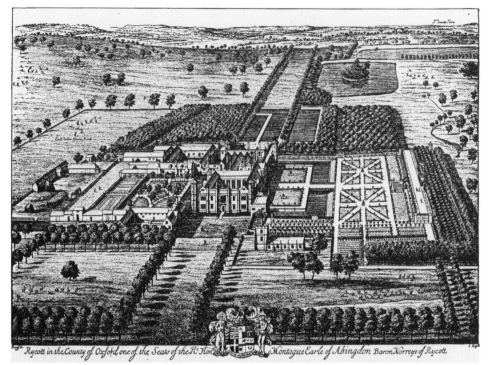

Rycott in the County of Oxford one of the Seats of the R.t Hon.ble Montague Earle of Abingdon Baron Norreys of Rycott

Rycote Park, Oxfordshire: the moated, early sixteenth-century house was burnt down in 1745 although fragments remain in use as a smaller house. The Kip engraving was made in 1714 and shows the rectangular garden layout extended into the surrounding countryside by avenues. The chapel, seen to the right and below the house, remains, and is in the care of English Heritage.

There were boscages of lilac and philadelphus.' Among the sculptures were a sundial and figures of a gardener and his wife 'both accoutred to their callings'. These were all carved by Nicholas Stone, a further link with the garden at Oxford.

Here both house and garden were designed as a single composition and the house was planned centrally within the garden with vistas extending through both. Immediately by the house was a wilderness of shrubs and fruit trees. Either side of this gates led out into long walks, terminated at the ends near the house by statues of Hercules and Antaeus and Cain and Abel. It was between these two walks that the largest feature of the garden was sited. This was a large bowling green with a walk around it and with a line of cypress trees around the whole. Beyond this bowling green area there was a curious trench-like feature which led down to a grotto containing a well and with a brick building above which served as a banqueting house, with access to the roof, from which one might look down on the garden. Contemporaries remarked especially upon the way in which the view on entering was restricted so that one only appreciated the garden gradually as one wandered through it and came upon the alternation of closed and open effects.

Aubrey has also provided a description of the other garden made by Sir John, at Lavington in Wiltshire. He emphasises the use made of elevations and depressions or irregularities and that views of the surrounding countryside could be had from the south side of the garden. A fine clear stream through the length of the garden had several statues set in it. The exploitation of irregularities in the ground and of views outwards from the garden suggests the stirrings of tendencies that were later to emerge in the landscape garden of the following century. That these should have been recognised as of Italian inspiration is not without interest.

The Italian gardens of Caroline England

From these gardens developed the typical form of the garden of Caroline England. The layout was essentially simple when compared to that of the Jacobean garden, with a classical simplicity aiming at a monumental effect, and with both house and garden related, usually both sharing the same centre lines to their symmetrical design. The elements would have a four-square rectangular design and usually there would be a raised terrace along the side opposite to the house. This terrace might incorporate a banqueting house, a grotto or an arcade or a combination of these and the terrace might extend along the sides of the garden as well as along the end.

Gardens of this type were laid out at Temple Newsam, West Yorkshire; at Rycote, Oxfordshire; at Much Hadham, Hertfordshire; and at Durdans, Surrey. At none of these places does any trace of such gardens remain today. All these gardens are, however, familiar to us from the engravings of Kip and Knyff and, indeed, it is through their eyes that we tend to view the great gardens of the period.

Royal gardens

Charles I's queen, Henrietta Maria, brought with her from France a taste for gardens and brought over too André Mollet, who was to become the dominating figure of the Caroline garden. André was a younger son of Claude Mollet, and a member of a whole line of gardeners connected with the royal gardens of France. He visited England twice, on both occasions in the service of the Queen. In 1629-33 he laid out the gardens of St James's Palace in London and in 1642 he laid out those at Wimbledon House near London.

The gardens at St James's Palace were in two separate walled enclosures either side of the single great court and related to the two suites

Groombridge Place, Kent, where the house of the mid seventeenth century stands within an older moat.

of apartments intended for the use of the king and the queen. Each had parterres bordered by box hedges; one had flowers around the walls and the other seems to have had walks beneath fruit trees. One had a long covered gallery with sculptures of stone and bronze. In addition there was a museum garden displaying part of Charles I's extensive collection of sculptures. Although no pictorial representation of these gardens has survived, the impression given by descriptions left by visitors is of a modest scheme on a considerably lesser scale than the gardens of Wilton that were being laid out at the same time.

The other schemes carried out on the royal gardens consisted of alterations to existing gardens such as those of Somerset House, London, where two new fountains were added along with new statuary. The well known Diana or Arethusa Fountain by Francesco Fanelli that now stands in Bushy Park, Middlesex, was an important addition to the Privy Garden. At the Queen's House, Greenwich, London, work was in progress in 1636 and during the same year John Tradescant, the gardener at Oatlands, the Queen's house in Surrey, was busy altering the garden there, including making an orange garden. In 1637 Inigo Jones designed paintings for the walls there, presumably *trompe-l'oeil* simulated landscapes, and this sort of decoration was a conscious revival of a popular feature of gardens of the ancient world.

The Queen's Garden within the Royal Botanic Gardens, Kew, Surrey: modern interpretation of a seventeenth-century garden.

Wimbledon

Wimbledon House had been built by the Cecil family and was purchased for the Queen in 1639. Inigo Jones was called in to improve the house and André Mollet was recalled from France to lay out a new garden. The intention behind the new layout was to get rid of the by now old-fashioned Mannerist clutter and irregularity of a series of enclosed gardens and to replace them with a unified symmetrical design about a central vista from the main door to the steps leading from the lower to the upper gardens. Immediately before the main south façade of the house was a terrace with summerhouses either end and four square knots, the two inner ones centred on fountains, the outer ones centred on cypress trees. Around this lower garden was a rail painted white with spikes in the corners and a row of cypress trees. Then, on a higher level, came a pleached lime walk with a wooden banqueting house each end and beyond this a wilderness on one side and a maze on the other. Still further beyond these features was a private walk edged with thorn and with summerhouses either end. To the east was the orange garden with four parterres of flowers bordered with box and with turf between. There were sixty orange trees in tubs disposed about the garden, six pomegranate trees and a lemon tree, and with a garden house where they were all kept during the winter.

Packwood House, Warwickshire: the yews often said to form an allegory of the Sermon on the Mount, but in fact planted during the nineteenth century.

Wimbledon was therefore a transitional design. There were signs of the new developments that were to come to fruition after the Civil War with the development of the baroque garden. Wimbledon was of modest size, for the condition of the royal purse hardly permitted anything more extensive, and its design was somewhat tentative and backward looking. That Mollet was called upon to design the garden is indicative of the dominating influence of the French in European garden design, an influence that was to grow all the stronger during the following century. The Mollet family worked in Germany and Sweden as well as in France and England and throughout western Europe it was French design that was looked upon as the ideal to aim at in the making of gardens.

The garden of allegory

The making of gardens during the early seventeenth century was no mere exercise in horticulture and design. There were elaborate allegorical overtones throughout a great garden and the theme of the garden as a microcosm of creation was perhaps the most important of all. The garden has a perpetual sequence of birth, growth, death and resurrection which reflects that of the larger creation of the Almighty, the universe itself. Moreover in a country now bereft of monastic cloisters the garden was the place for contemplation and one could meditate in a garden house perhaps better than anywhere else in Stuart England. The most obvious manifestation of this religious attitude to gardens is the creation of gardens based upon the Sermon on the Mount. The garden at Packwood, Warwickshire, is a mid nineteenth-century replanting of a seventeenth-century garden but the yews representing Jesus, the Twelve Apostles and the multitude are a fascinating reminder of an attitude to garden making now lost to us.

In addition to this religious allegory the garden had what was to become an even more persuasive interest. The garden was the place where those of a philosophical disposition, or even a merely intellectual disposition, might affect the fashionable attitude to life of melancholy. Those who wished to appear before the world as intellectuals would have their portrait painted in a garden. Perhaps even more tellingly, they might be depicted outside a garden contemplating the world without but with a reminder of the humanist version of the environment within the confines of the garden. The ordered, tidy world of the garden contrasted with the wild, romantic world of untamed nature outside.

Bolsover

All these Caroline gardens have long since vanished save one. At Bolsover Castle in Derbyshire William Cavendish, Earl of Newcastle, created a curious pseudo-Gothic castle and alongside it a small walled garden centred upon an elaborate fountain of Venus. Both castle and garden survive today and were designed around a complex allegorical scheme with the garden as a garden of love. It was in this garden that, on 30th July 1634, Charles I and Henrietta Maria walked after being welcomed by Cavendish on their return from their progress in Scotland and it was here that they attended the masque *Love's Welcome to Bolsover* by Ben Jonson. The theme of the masque was that of courtly love, perhaps an ironic epilogue to a period during which the King had ruled by divine right and without a parliament and which was so soon to end in the turmoil of civil war.

Botanical gardeners

The outstanding gardener of the times was John Tradescant the Younger (1608-62), son of the outstanding gardener of Jacobean times. He too went plant collecting and was busy in Virginia at the time of his father's death in 1637. On his return he succeeded his father as gardener to Queen Henrietta Maria and carried on his father's activities at The Ark in Lambeth, London, where, besides a physic garden, he collected a great range of 'curiosities'. In 1656 he published a catalogue of these collections which details plants from as far afield as Persia, Barbados, China and North Africa, as well as North America, which had by then become more or less accepted as a source of botanical rarities. When John the Younger died the collections at Lambeth were purchased by Elias Ashmole, who presented them to Oxford University, where they formed the nucleus of the Ashmolean Museum, the oldest museum in Britain. Although the site of their physic garden at Lambeth has been long since built over, both Tradescants were buried in the churchyard of St Mary's church, Lambeth, and their joint tomb is preserved in the garden that surrounds the now disused church, which has become the Museum of Garden History and where the memory of the Tradescants is much honoured.

Another gardener who deserves to be remembered is Jacob Bobart (1599-1679), who served as gardener for the Oxford Botanic Garden. His catalogue of the plants there of 1648 lists some 1600 species and varieties being cultivated in spite of the Civil War going on around him in the city, which served as the Royalist capital for much of the war.

Thomas Johnson (1600-44) was the herbalist who is credited with having imported the first bananas seen in Britain. His greatest claim to being remembered by posterity is, however, his corrected edition of Gerard's *Herbal* of 1643. He died in the defence of Basing Castle in Hampshire during the Civil War. An ardent Royalist too was Robert Morison (1620-83), a Scot, who served in the Royalist armies and followed Charles II to France, becoming professor of botany at Oxford after the Restoration.

Scottish gardening

During the seventeenth century there developed in Scotland a distinctive type of garden that subsequent centuries have certainly come to regard as essentially Scottish. This is the walled garden, sometimes detached from the house, but planted with herbs and flowers and sometimes ornamented with a sundial or other sculptural feature. The restored garden at Edzell Castle, Tayside, with its elaborately decorated walls, is the best known example but the simpler one at Aberdour Castle, Fife, is notable and is presently under restoration.

Such gardens, usually of quite modest dimensions, were being made throughout Scotland well into the eighteenth century. In 1683 John Reid, in *The Scots Gardener*, the first book on gardening published in Scotland, set out requirements for good gardening in the Scottish climate. In addition he urged his countrymen to aim for grandeur in their gardens by emphasising the importance of an impressive layout and an orderly arrangement of the various parts of the garden. Above all Reid insisted upon the importance of regularity in the design.

Such strict standards were not likely to be universally popular and the work of Andrew Fletcher of Saltoun, Lothian, is probably more typical.

Edzell Castle, Tayside: the knot garden within the walls, originally laid out in 1604 by Sir David Lindsay, Lord Edzell.

The plan of his garden at Saltoun is a series of rectangular enclosures set out with little concern for the overall effect or design. His method of bringing them into some sort of relationship was the novel one of providing *clairvoyées* in the surrounding walls so that the central features of each garden could be seen from each other. There was thus an irregular pattern imposed upon the design which could have a degree of openness without losing the shelter of the walls so important in the Scottish climate.

The gardens laid out by Sir William Bruce (*c*.1630-1710) were more architectural in character than those of either Reid or Fletcher. At Balcaskie, Fife, he took advantage of the steeply sloping site with the splendid prospect of the Firth of Forth to lay out a series of three terraces forming at the same time a large enclosed rectangle. On the other side of the house he created a garden in which the inevitable irregularities are balanced either side of the design by the subsidiary buildings to provide the grand approach he felt to be essential to a great house. The resulting sequence of court, house and garden was given further point by the fact that the Bass Rock in the distant Forth was 'arranged' to be on the centre line of the whole symmetrical layout.

The use of a distant landmark as a focal point of the design is one

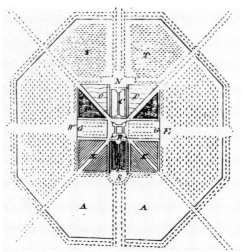

(Left) The ideal Scottish garden, as illustrated in John Reid's 'The Scots Gardener' of 1683.

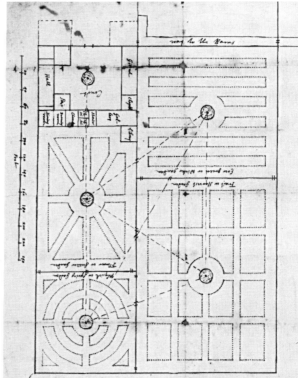

(Right) The garden of Saltoun Hall, Lothian, as shown in a plan by Fletcher of Saltoun. (Royal Commission on Ancient and Historical Monuments of Scotland, by kind permission of Dr W. Brogden.)

Old Yester House, Gifford, Lothian: a painting by de Witt, about 1700, of the garden laid out for the Marquess of Tweedale. (Royal Commission on Ancient and Historical Monuments of Scotland, by kind permission of Gian Carlo Menotti.)

which became a feature of gardens designed by Bruce. At Kinross, Tayside, the ruined castle on the island in Loch Leven is the focal point and at Hopetoun, Lothian, there is a choice of the ruined Blackness Castle for a day of Scottish mist or the distant prospect of North Berwick Law for a clear day. This introduction of a feature of the distant landscape into the design of the garden was far in advance of general practice anywhere in the two kingdoms at the time and suggests a feeling for the landscape which was to lead to the development of the landscape garden during the following century.

For all this, there is little evidence at this period, of the prowess of Scottish gardeners as plantsmen, which was later to be so conspicuous. Sir Robert Sibbald (1641-1722), returning to Scotland after medical study overseas, certainly regarded his native land as being backward in this respect.

Sir Thomas Hanmer

The disturbed state of the times caused not a few men to retire to such obscurity as they could muster and devote themselves to the innocent pursuit of gardening. Such a one was Sir Thomas Hanmer (1612-78), whose *Garden Book* of 1659 described choice plants with directions for their cultivation in the British climate. He retired to his home in Flintshire (now Clwyd) when war threatened but before that he had travelled on the continent and collected a circle of friends that included all the notable gardeners of the day.

In his book he remarks upon the great improvements in gardening that had occurred during his time. The rather cosy enclosed feel of gardens of his youth was being replaced by a spacious stateliness. A new feature was the vista, even if it was rather limited in extent at this time. There was now a tendency to keep garden features low when close to the house so that the view from within the rooms was not obstructed. Hedges and knots would be quite low and fruit trees and the like were kept well away from the house. Beyond would be the parterres, 'as the French call them', and between would be alleys of gravel. Further away from the house were 'compartments' and borders of flowers which would often be set within grass and the whole ornamented with vases or specimen evergreens.

Other features might be thickets for birds, labyrinths of hedges or fountains or cascades. True devotees of floristry might have a private garden where they might grow their special treasures 'such as are not to be exposed to every one's view' and there might be a winter house for plants. This would be very different from the greenhouse as it evolved in later years and would be just a large building with windows on the south side warmed by a stove or coals in a pan in cold weather. The use of hotbeds, made with dung or fermenting brewers' hops, was well understood. There must have been many fairly modest gardens of this kind and traces of many remain today.

Hanmer gives extensive lists of plants grown in gardens of his time and the cultural instructions he gives are, in general, very sound. He was obviously much concerned with fruit growing and with 'greens'. These were shrubs grown for their foliage, and a delight in growing a varied range of 'greens' was to become increasingly important in future years.

The writings of Hanmer give ample evidence of the rapidly developing interest in the introduction of new plants from overseas. One important reason for this was that improved techniques of cultivation were making it possible to grow tender plants in Britain that would formerly have been impossible. Many of these plants were described by the vague term 'Indian', which could be applied to any plant from exotic countries overseas.

Sir William Temple and Moor Park

Among the most famous descriptions of any English garden is that of Moor Park near Farnham, Surrey, recalled by Sir William Temple (1628-99) in his *Upon the Gardens of Epicurus* of 1685. After a career as a statesman he remembered the garden he knew as a youth:

> 'Because I take the garden I have named, to have been in all kinds the most beautiful and perfect, at least in the figure and disposition, that I have ever seen, I will describe it for a model to those that meet with such a situation, and are above the regards of common expense. It lies on the side of a hill (upon which the house stands) but not very steep. The length of the house, where the best rooms, and of most use or pleasure, lies upon the breadth of the garden, the great parlour opens into the middle of a gravel-walk that lies even with it, and which may be as I remember about three hundred paces long, and broad in proportion, the border set with standard laurels, and at large distances, which have the beauty of orange-trees out of flower and fruit; from the walk are three descents by many stone steps in the middle and at each end, into a very large parterre. This is divided into quarters by gravel walks, and adorned with two fountains and eight statues in the several quarters; at the end of the terrace walk are two summer houses, and the sides of the parterre are ranged with two large cloisters, which are paved with stone, and designed for walks of shade, there being none other in the whole parterre. Over these two cloisters are two terraces covered with lead and fenced with balusters, and the passage into these airy walks is out of the two summer houses at the end of the first terrace walk. The cloister facing south is covered with vines, and would have been proper for an orange-house, and the other for myrtles, or other more common greens, and had, I doubt not, been cast for that purpose, if this piece of gardening had been then in as much vogue as it is now.

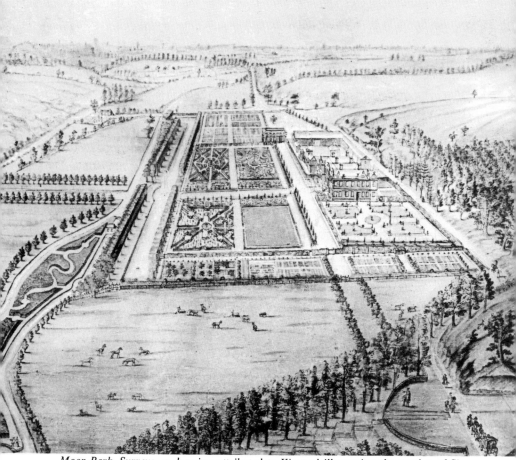

Moor Park, Surrey: a drawing attributed to Kip and illustrating the garden of Sir William Temple at the end of the seventeenth century. (Surrey Local Studies Library.)

'From the middle of this parterre is a descent by many steps flying on each side of a grotto that lies between them (covered with lead and flat) into the lower garden, which is all fruit-trees ranged about the several quarters of a wilderness which is very shady; the walks here are all green, the grotto embellished with figures of shell rock-work, fountains and water works. If the hill had not ended with the lower garden, and the wall were not bounded by a common way that goes through the park, they might have added a third quarter of all greens; but this want is supplied by a garden on the other side of the house, which is all of that sort, very wild, shady, and adorned with rough rock-work and fountains.'

Late Stuart gardens

The period of the Commonwealth and the Puritan ascendancy was not a time of progress in the arts, and garden making, so dependent upon settled conditions, was no exception. With the restoration of the monarchy, in the person of Charles II, in 1660, activity began once more.

This was thus a period when, all over England, country houses were being surrounded by impressive gardens. The design would be aligned about a central avenue which formed a vista directed towards the centre of the symmetrical façade of the house. Either side were parterres set out in flowing patterns rather like those of a Paisley shawl and at right angles to the main axis there were cross-axes each terminated with some building, sculpture or other object of interest. Within this basically rectangular pattern there might be enclosures, or bosquets, formed by hedges and within these bosquets might be contrasting flower gardens, viewpoints, sculptures, garden buildings or other delights.

A particularly frequent feature is the *patte d'oie* or goose-foot layout, where several avenues or other types of vista radiate from a single point — usually the centre point of the garden façade of the house. If many such avenues radiated in this way a stellar pattern might result and in the largest and grandest layouts a whole series of star-shaped designs might be created, producing a series of triangles between the radiating avenues. Then there were the quincunxes, patterns of closely spaced trees, as well as the grottoes and cascades familiar from earlier gardens.

Much of the space in these gardens was taken up by stretches of water and by woodland. Indeed sometimes the garden groves seemed to have been carved out of solid woodland. Water was used as simple rectangular expanses and the elaborate fountains and cascades of the French garden at home are much less in evidence in Britain.

Le Nôtre

Much the most famous of French garden designers, and perhaps of all garden designers, was André Le Nôtre (1613-1700). He was born into gardening, being the son of the head gardener to the French kings. Such was his fame that innumerable gardens laid out in anything even faintly resembling a French style are attributed to him. He dominated European garden design, both during his lifetime and for a century afterwards.

There were frequent invitations for him to travel to design gardens outside France and Charles II of England asked him to work at Greenwich. He appears to have prepared plans in France and left the execution of the design on the ground to John Rose, one of the Royal Gardeners. John Rose and the other Royal Gardener, George London, visited Le Nôtre to learn from him.

John Evelyn

The marked interest in the planting of trees during this period was inevitable as a consequence of the enthusiasm for the French garden. Previously there had been a tendency to look upon trees as something provided by the bounty of nature — one did not have to plant trees; they grew anyway unless one stopped them doing so. The change in thinking was to a great extent due to the advocacy of John Evelyn (1620-1706), polymath and founder member of the Royal Society in 1662. One of the early concerns of the Society was the shortage of timber suitable for shipbuilding and Evelyn was asked to report on the problem. From his paper, presented to the Society, he wrote his *Sylva, or a Discourse of Forest Trees* and this book became the standard work on trees for at least the following century. He advocated the planting of trees everywhere and the traditional belief that someone who plants a tree is a benefactor to mankind in general can be traced back to Evelyn. He was not concerned only with the planting of trees to maintain a supply of shipbuilding timber but advocated with passionate zeal that trees were an embellishment of any well managed estate and ought to be the concern of any responsible landowner. Evergreen trees were a particular delight of his and he popularised the planting of yew, holly and cedar of Lebanon, although he was by no means the first to plant any of them.

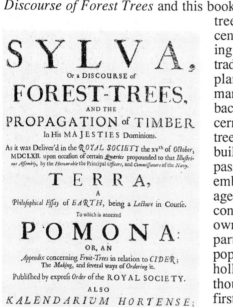

Evelyn also wrote of fruit-tree growing in his *Pomona, or an Appendix Concerning Fruit-Trees in Relation to Cider*, in which, besides advocating greater activity in the fruit garden, he set out the advantages of the careful selection of good strains of fruit. In 1664 he published *Kalendarium Hortense: or the Gardener's Almanack, Directing what he is to do monthly*

Title page of the third edition of John Evelyn's 'Sylva', 1679, a book which had an immense influence in stimulating the planting of trees throughout Britain.

throughout the year, and what fruits and flowers are in prime, surely the forerunner of the numerous monthly gardening calendars that are still such a feature of bookstalls and television gardening series. In later editions all three works were bound together and in this form the book is to be found in innumerable country house libraries, for Evelyn wrote for the educated landowner rather than for the humble gardener. Books intended for the latter were still a thing of the future.

JOANNES EVELYN ARMIG.
REG. SOCIETATIS SOC.

John Rea

Evelyn was concerned mainly with the big issues of what trees to plant and why. For the details of cultivation and layout perhaps a more informative source of information is John Rea (*floruit* 1665-70), about whose life little is known but who has left us his *Flora seu de Florum Cultura* of 1665, his only literary work.

John Evelyn: portrait by Sir Godfrey Kneller. Evelyn was the dominant figure in gardening in England during the later seventeenth century. (The Royal Society.)

Here we find instruction about the detailed layout of the simpler type of gardens becoming usual in his day. He advocated two rectangular walled gardens, the one nearer the house being for flowers and the further one being for fruit, but both for 'delight, recreation and entertainment'.

Rea refers to the beds in his garden as 'parterres' and by this time the French term seems finally to have ousted the older term 'knot'. He writes of 'frets' planted with flowers such as martagons, crown imperials and other tall plants in the corners and paeonies in 'tufts' in the centre with dwarf plants around them such as tulips, irises and anemones. There should be a summerhouse with chairs for sitting out and outside the walled gardens there should be a nursery garden complete with hotbeds of fermenting material such as dung or tanners' bark.

Rea goes on to review the plants available to gardeners in his day and, like most writers of the time, gives much space to 'greens'. These are evergreen shrubs and his favourites seem to have been the phillyrea and the strawberry-tree but he also loved honeysuckles, jasmines and clematis. Much space was inevitably given to bulbs, especially to tulips

A plan for 'a magnificent garden all upon a level' from 'The Theory and Practice of Gardening', a translation by John James of a work by Alexander Le Blond, 1728.

St Paul's Walden Bury, Hertfordshire: the three radiating rides lined with beech hedges which form the basis of the woodland garden laid out by Edward Gilbert c.1725-30.

since the tulip was at the peak of its popularity in his day. Auriculas too get much attention and he writes also of lychnis, wallflower, primroses, cowslips and oxlips. Then there are 'gillyflowers' of various kinds such as the queen's gillyflower (*Hesperis matronalis*), the stock gillyflower (*Lucoium luteum*), which we know as the wallflower, and the gillyflower (*Dianthus caryophyllus*), the flower known to us as the carnation. The names of plants, and their spelling, were somewhat vague in the seventeenth century.

Rea has a second book of his work on summer and autumn plants such as delphiniums, cornflowers, lupins, sweet peas and scabious. His third book deals with the fruit garden, describing twenty kinds of apples and twenty pears. Five kinds of quince are mentioned and he writes of 24 kinds of cherry and 44 plums. He describes six apricots, 35 peaches and also mentions the nectarine, fig, mulberry and cornelian cherry.

The kind of garden for which Rea wrote was the middling kind of garden, well below the great gardens of the houses of the aristocracy, yet much larger than the cottage gardens of such of the lower classes as were fortunate enough to have a garden of any kind. His type of simple rectangular walled enclosure must have been very common attached to the newly built houses of the rising middle class of the late seventeenth and early eighteenth centuries. They remained in vogue for such houses long after their grander brethren had been 'landscaped' by the fashionable practitioners of the landscape garden school of design. Indeed, they survive still where successive owners were content to ignore changing fashions in garden design and to carry on in the old ways.

Royal gardening

On being restored to his throne after his 'travels' it was natural that Charles II should set about recreating the gardens of the royal palaces and that this work should be greatly under French influence. Charles had had much contact with matters French during the previous few years and during the last decades of the seventeenth century French influence triumphed, but not only in England — all Europe aimed to garden in the French manner.

It seems that the first of the royal parks to be given attention was St James's Park in London, where André and Gabriel Mollet, as newly appointed gardeners to the King, were set to work laying out long straight walks lined with acacias. Unfortunately these trees proved unable to withstand the winds, which broke off many of the branches, and they were soon cut down and replaced. There was a long, canal-like water feature 2800 feet (853 metres) long by 100 feet (30 metres) wide, with walks radiating from a semicircle of trees before steps to Whitehall Palace. The canal was well stocked with waterfowl. These were a special delight of the King and thus continued the association of St James's Park with exotic animals and birds from earlier times.

There has long been a tradition that Le Nôtre himself prepared the designs for the new layout of St James's Park. Possibly the Mollets were able to obtain a design from the great man. If he prepared any plans they have long since vanished and it seems more likely that the design was by the Mollets working under the general influence of Le Nôtre.

The Mollets were also kept busy at Hampton Court, where an even longer canal was dug aligned on the balcony of the Queen's apartments. As at St James's there were walks radiating from a semicircle of trees but the scale was much greater. The canal at Hampton Court remains today, unlike the one at St James's Park, which was reshaped during the nineteenth century, and one can still gaze along its vast length towards Kingston-upon-Thames.

John Rose

The influence of Le Nôtre continued under John Rose (c.1621-77) since, as a young man, Rose was sent to work under him at Versailles by the Earl of Essex. On returning, he became gardener at Essex House, the Earl's London house, until he took up his royal appointment at St James's. He was chiefly known as a skilled horticulturalist and if he was responsible for any of the design work at St James's Park it would have been much in the formal manner of the French tradition. He is now best remembered as the gardener seen presenting a pineapple to Charles II in the well known painting by Henry Danckerts.

'Mr Rose, the Royal Gardener, presenting to King Charles II the first pineapple raised in England': a painting by Henry Danckerts. (Victoria and Albert Museum.)

This painting is known in several versions as well as in engravings but it raises a number of doubts since the pineapple is not known to have been grown in England until later in the century and there are no written records of any occasion when the King was presented with a pineapple by Rose, or anyone else for that matter. So notable an event would surely have occasioned some reference in contemporary records.

The Restoration garden

The settlement of political affairs following the disruption of the Commonwealth period offered ideal conditions for the newly wealthy to create great houses and gardens suited to their improved status in the realm. There was thus much activity in gardening on the grand scale and this was accompanied by a great deal of restoration and improvement work by those members of the pre-Civil War aristocracy who had emerged from the late troubles with at least some of their estates, as well as their heads.

Cassiobury, near Watford in Hertfordshire, was among these great gardens, designed by Moses Cook for the Earl of Essex and notable for the avenues of wild cherry as well as fine woods. Cassiobury has now largely perished beneath the suburbs of Watford but another great garden, Chatsworth in Derbyshire, happily remains and in the hands of the Dukes of Devonshire, for whose ancestors it was created.

There are only traces of the garden made at Chatsworth during the Restoration period but paintings show the elaborate design based upon rectangular compartments with numerous water features, including fountains and the famous copper willow tree which spurted water from its branches. Travellers duly reported these marvels but remarked even more upon their surprise at finding this Elysium in the midst of the bare and barren moors of the Peak District. Even the immediate surround-

Chatsworth, Derbyshire: the vast extent of the garden layout of the end of the seventeenth century. This was virtually all swept away during the landscaping operations of 'Capability' Brown a century later.

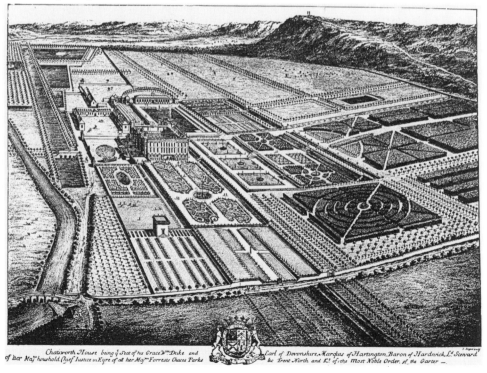

Chatsworth House being ȳ Seat of his Grace Ẇ™ Duke and of her Maȳ houshold Chief Iustice in Eyre of all her Maȳ™ Forrests Chaces Parks &c *Earl of Devonshire, Marquis of Hartington, Baron of Hardwick Lᵈ Steward &c Trent North and Kᵗ of the Most Noble Order of the Garter —*

ings of the great garden were largely devoid of trees. The vast planting programme put in hand at that time and continued ever since has resulted in both park and gardens being embowered in trees, although the contrast with the surrounding open moorland can still cause something of a shock.

Kirby Hall

The great gardens laid out at Kirby Hall in Northamptonshire are being restored for the second time. The gardens were already famous during the late seventeenth century but under Lord Hatton (1635 to *c.*1705) two large rectangular gardens were laid out to the west of the house, surrounded by raised terraces, and further south was a long wilderness of trees laid out to a pattern. Excavations in the 1930s uncovered a good deal of the stone edging which outlined the beds and the garden was restored, although not with authentic planting. Research and excavation has continued and in 1991 English Heritage began extensive work to raise the beds and paths from 4 to 6 inches (100 to 150 mm) to their original level. Eventually the beds will be replanted to a scheme based upon research into the Hatton archives. Excavation continues over much of the site.

The Scottish Restoration garden

Whilst there were great gardens around the great houses of Scotland there was a dearth of those lesser houses that, in England, were usually provided with a modest garden. All this was to change greatly during the following century but Scottish gardening as a craft was rapidly developing during the years following the Restoration.

In 1670, on the initiative of Sir Robert Sibbald (1641-1722), a plot of land near Holyrood Palace in Edinburgh was purchased for a physic garden to enable plants to be grown for teaching purposes in the medical school for which Edinburgh was already famous but also in an endeavour to raise the standards of cultivation of plants in Scotland. Sibbald had been in Paris and Leiden studying medicine and had been appalled by the poor standard of gardening among his fellow countrymen on his return. The little garden at Holyrood was the ancestor of the Royal Botanic Garden which flourishes in Edinburgh today.

Such gardens as existed in Scotland during this period were usually around the great houses and in design were little different from those to be found in England. On such estates there was much activity in tree planting since the bare nature of the countryside was an invariable source of comment by travellers until well into the following century. The view among Scotsmen previously had been that corn and oats were more important than trees and the revolution in attitude to trees in

Powis Castle, Powys: the terraced garden constructed about 1700.

The fine gatepiers at Canons Ashby, Northamptonshire, before the early eighteenth-century garden.

Hampton Court Palace, Middlesex: the Great Fountain Garden.

Hampton Court Palace, Middlesex: the Long Water.

Scotland took many years to percolate downwards from the aristocracy to the small landowners.

When, at length, the modest middling type of Scottish garden did develop, it has tended to remain unaltered as the vogue for landscaping was much less prevalent in Scotland than further south.

Plant introductions

The tide of plant introductions from distant parts of the world was already flowing strongly during the latter half of the seventeenth century. The European centre for the collections of such plants tended to be France and in particular the Jardin de Plantes. Such plants came especially from the eastern Mediterranean area and from North America. Throughout the period French influence was supreme but Holland was fast catching up and Dutch trading interests with far-flung parts of the world resulted in plants being brought to Amsterdam from India, Spain and the western Mediterranean area. From Paris and Amsterdam plants would be propagated and then find their way into the gardens of such wealthy British gardeners as were 'curious' in rare plants.

This rather circuitous process of plant introductions was by no means the only way new plants reached British gardens. There were certainly direct introductions by British traders. In the days prior to plant hygiene regulations such importations would usually be unrecorded and the activities of the Reverend Edward Pococke (1604-91) leave no doubt that important plants could reach Britain in this way. He is always credited with the introduction of the cedar of Lebanon, which he raised in his garden at Childrey, now in Oxfordshire, where he became rector after he had left his post as chaplain to the merchants at Aleppo in Syria.

Then there would be seeds sent home by friends and relations of British gardeners travelling abroad or who were temporarily working overseas. Besides Bishop Henry Compton, always anxious to find rare plants for his garden at Fulham Palace, London, there were Sir Hans Sloane and many another lesser known plant fancier on the lookout for intriguing plants. The great age of plant hunters, who were sent out expressly to look for rare plants, was yet to come but already in the 1690s one of the gardeners at Hampton Court, John Road, was sent across the Atlantic to Virginia to collect plants, being paid £234 11s 9d for his pains.

Many of these newly introduced plants were tender when grown in the British climate and developments in the design of greenhouses were soon required to enable such 'exoticks' to be grown in Britain. Until the end of the seventeenth century a greenhouse was just a room in which to keep 'greens', tender shrubs in tubs or pots, during the winter. It might be equipped with a stove, brazier or other open fire to give some protection from the worst of frosts but otherwise the plants looked after themselves.

Gradually it began to be realised that the fumes given off by the open fires and stoves were more damaging to the plants than frosts. Indirect heating by means of flues passing under and through the walls of the greenhouse is first noted by John Evelyn in 1685 at the Apothecaries Garden at Chelsea, London, but soon afterwards a similar greenhouse was built at Hampton Court. This had several sections with stoves beneath them to provide heating.

John Evelyn was largely responsible for evolving an improved design of greenhouse, following discussions with such fellow members of the Royal Society as Robert Hooke and Sir Christopher Wren. In 1691 he published the results of his researches, emphasising the need to ensure a circulation of air within the greenhouse with warmed fresh air being continually admitted. He proposed that the furnace be sited outside, but adjoining, the greenhouse with several pipes passing above the furnace to admit warm air. The tainted air inside would be drawn off by means of a flue passing beneath the floor, through which the draught caused by the fire would ensure a circulation.

The trade of gardening

The rapid developments in gardening, and especially the greatly increased activity in garden making during the latter decades of the seventeenth century, resulted in a demand for the commercial supply of seeds, plants and other gardening requisites. Thus the business of the nurseryman became an accepted trade and a number of firms developed, mainly located close to the principal centres of population.

In the London area the Hoxton district, just to the north-east of the business and financial centre of the City, was the location of a number of these nurseryman businesses. Here was found George Ricketts, from whom Sir Thomas Hanmer bought plants. Captain Leonard Gurle specialised in fruit trees; the business of Pearson dealt in flowers and that of Darby in shrubs. Thomas Fairchild was especially famous: he was the author of *The City Gardener* of 1722, which was among the first publications to address the problems of small town gardens set in the smoke-ridden atmosphere of the rapidly increasing towns of the time. He did notable work in distributing newly introduced North American plants such as the tulip-tree and the catalpa and was a pioneer in experimenting with hybridisation.

There was another concentration of nurserymen in the Hammersmith and Fulham area to the west of London. Here were to be found the firm of Wrench, famous for their hollies, and that of Hermon Van Guine, who had been gardener to Catherine of Braganza, widow of Charles II,

Wrest Park, Bedfordshire. The Long Water was constructed between 1706 and 1740 on a vista linking the house with the pavilion designed by Thomas Archer.

The reconstructed seventeenth-century garden at Boscobel House, Shropshire, where Charles II hid in an oak tree to escape capture after the Battle of Worcester in 1651.

The design of the formal garden at Erddig, Clwyd, although laid out in the early eighteenth century, is more typical of the previous century.

Chelsea Physic Garden, London, dates from 1673, when it was founded by the Society of Apothecaries for providing herbs for medicinal purposes.

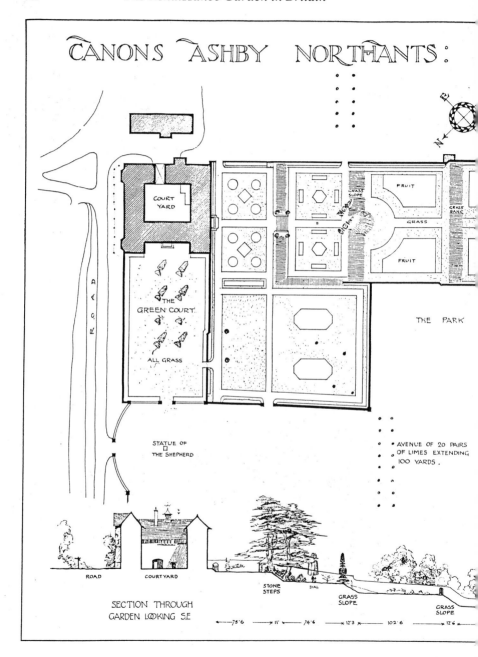

CANONS ASHBY NORTHANTS:

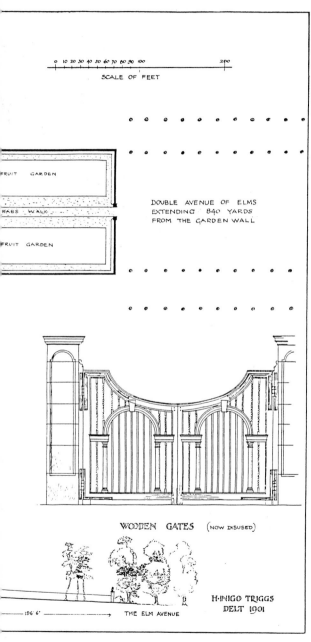

0 10 20 30 40 50 60 70 80 90 100   200

SCALE OF FEET

FRUIT   GARDEN

RAGS WALK

FRUIT GARDEN

DOUBLE AVENUE OF ELMS
EXTENDING   840 YARDS
FROM THE GARDEN WALL

WOODEN GATES (NOW DISUSED)

196' 6"

THE ELM AVENUE

H·INIGO TRIGGS
DELT 1901

Canons Ashby, Northamptonshire. The early eighteenth-
century garden has a series of
walled enclosures carefully
related to the gently sloping site
and surrounded by a small park.
After a period of neglect both
house and garden have been
restored by the National Trust.
The drawing by H. Inigo Triggs
shows the garden as surveyed
in 1901.

The formal garden at Shotover Park, Oxfordshire, begun in c.1718. The long canal links the house with a Gothic temple and there remain avenues and cross-walks on the other side of the house.

Pitmedden, Grampian, where the Great Garden, laid out by Sir Alexander Seton in the late seventeenth century, has been recreated by the National Trust for Scotland since 1952.

Drummond Castle, Tayside. The vast parterre was originally laid out c.1630 but its present form is due to a restoration and elaboration carried out in 1830.

Earlshall, Fife. The topiary garden laid out by Sir Robert Lorimer in the 1890s around the sixteenth-century tower house.

and who dealt in orange and lemon plants.

All these firms were probably quite small but in 1681 an altogether more ambitious enterprise was established. The moving spirit was George London (died 1713), who was gardener to Bishop Compton at Fulham Palace. Although of humble origins, he made a modest entry into great events during the revolution of 1688, when he assisted the escape of Princess Anne, which was organised by Bishop Compton and the Duchess of Marlborough. His other partners included William Looker, formerly gardener at Somerset House; Moses Cook, Gardener at Cassiobury, Hertfordshire; and Field of Woburn Abbey, Bedfordshire. Within a few years death or retirement had eliminated all these partners and by 1687 London had taken as partner Henry Wise (1653-1738). It was as London and Wise that the firm became the dominant force in English gardening until well into the following century. The 100 acres (40 ha) of their nursery was at Brompton, where now the museums of South Kensington cover their grounds. Such a large nursery was a new phenomenon at the time and it was from here that most of the plants required for the new gardens of the period were sent out. Wise concentrated on supervising the business at Brompton whilst London journeyed about Britain advising clients on the design of their gardens. Occasionally he journeyed overseas to France and Holland to visit gardens and nurseries. With the arrival of William and Mary jointly on the throne, London added the duties of royal gardener to his work in 1689.

Outside the London area there were doubtless gardeners on the large estates who supplied the more common seeds and fruit trees and the supply of seeds became a recognised subsidiary trade for corn chandlers. The choice available from local suppliers was, however, very limited and anything at all out of the usual had to be obtained from the London nurserymen. There is some evidence to suggest that a few provincial firms of greater scope had begun to develop in such places as York before the close of the seventeenth century but information about the scope of their trade is indirect and patchy at this early stage.

Williamite gardens

The new king, William III soon established himself as a great lover of gardens, being especially fond of evergreen shrubs, or 'greens' as they were known. The close ties with Holland enabled British gardeners to have access to the plants imported into Holland through their trade links with the east, especially the East Indies and Japan, and perhaps also to just a little of the gardening skills which Dutch gardeners had developed ahead of any other nation in Europe.

George London was appointed Master-Gardener and Deputy Superintendent of the Royal Gardens to the new king under William Bentinck as Superintendent. Bentinck was a Dutchman who came over as an intimate of the new king and was largely occupied with great matters of state, with London doing the actual garden work. After his retirement in 1700, however, Bentinck spent much time gardening and plants from his Dutch residence were sent over for the gardens at Hampton Court.

A further innovation under William and Mary was the vogue for lead figures as garden ornaments. The leading supplier was Jan van Nost, yet another Dutchman, who had a factory in the Haymarket in London where he produced figures to order which still embellish many a fine garden. The fashion was to paint the figures in lifelike colours, not a practice appealing to present-day taste, but one which the visitor should bear in mind sometimes when looking at such garden statuary.

Denham Place, Buckinghamshire. The axial garden is remarkable for the profusion of sculpture. A view probably of c.1695. (Yale Center for British Art, Paul Mellon Collection.)

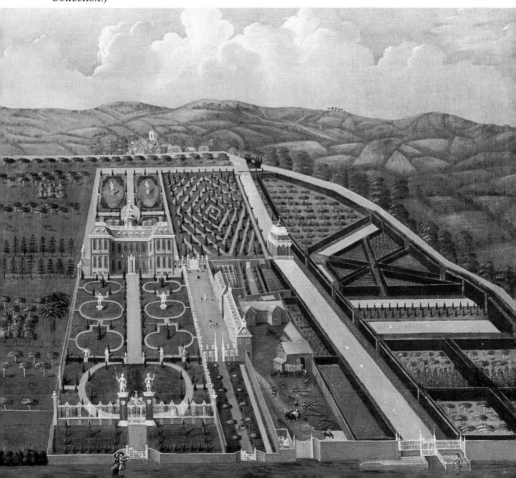

The parterre at Oxburgh Hall, Norfolk, said to have been copied from a French design about 1845.

The Tudor-style garden constructed at the Tudor House Museum, Southampton.

(Left) Althorp, Northamptonshire. In the park a series of stone pedestals records the dates of tree plantings between 1567 and 1901, an early example of historicism.

(Right) The parterre at Holme Pierrepont Hall, Nottinghamshire, probably laid out shortly after 1852.

(Below) Broughton Castle, Oxfordshire: the knot garden of box and roses laid out within the walls of the old kitchen garden.

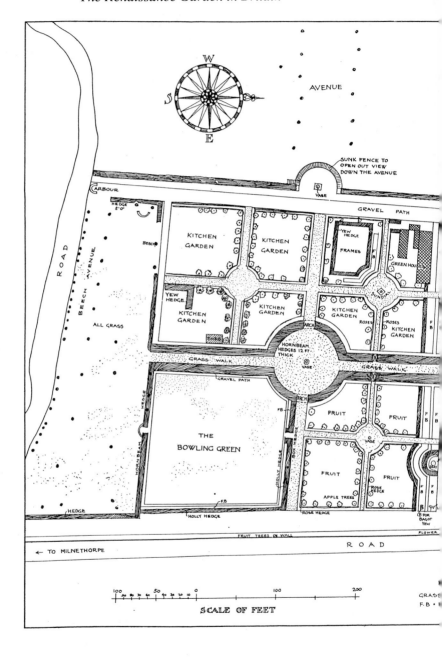

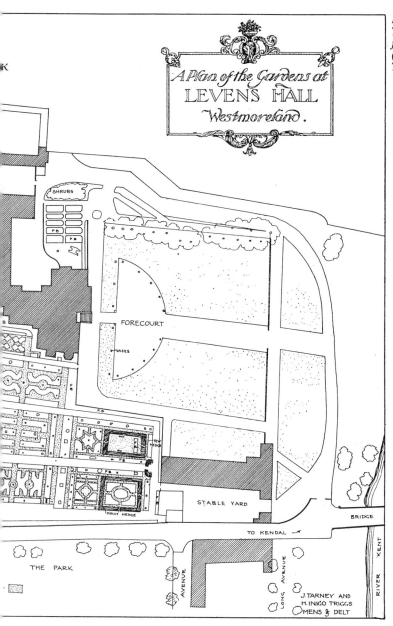

Levens Hall, Cumbria. The layout of the famous topiary garden. (Drawing by H. Inigo Triggs.)

Pierrepont House, Nottinghamshire. The garden layout of a grand town house, c.1705, complete with a profusion of flower pots. (Yale Center for British Art, Paul Mellon Collection.)

Hampton Court is probably the best known of the gardens of the reign of William and Mary. This is as it should be for it was William's favourite palace and it was before Wren's great east front that George London created the semicircular fountain garden which is still such a great feature of the gardens. The vast parterre was centred upon the axis of the Long Water, the canal dug in 1661 for Charles II and within the semicircle of trees planted then. Two additional avenues were now added either side of the central one in which the canal was set. The enormous parterre had all manner of intricate patterns set out in the beds with numerous fountains, statues and specimen yews. The water supply for the fountains always seems to have given trouble and the fountains were soon reduced to the central one. The beds are now much simplified but the yews are still there, now grown to sizes never envisaged by the original designer.

Hampton Court has frequently been referred to as the outstanding example of both the French and the Dutch influence upon English garden design. Both influences are certainly to be discerned for the vast avenues are French in inspiration as the intricacy of the parterre and the importance of evergreen shrubs and sculpture are Dutch.

For such great avenues to be seen to full effect reasonably level ground was required and this condition was frequently absent in Britain. One conspicuous example of this was at Powis Castle, Powys, in Wales, where the cousin of William III, the Earl of Rochford, created the magnificent series of terraces from the natural face of the rock on which the castle stands. There is, perhaps, as much of the inspiration of the great Italian gardens here as of those of Holland but there were in

Hampton Court, Herefordshire, as painted, possibly by Jan Stevens c.1706-10: the elaborate, formal design of the period just before the fashion for landscaping. (Yale Center for British Art, Paul Mellon Collection.)

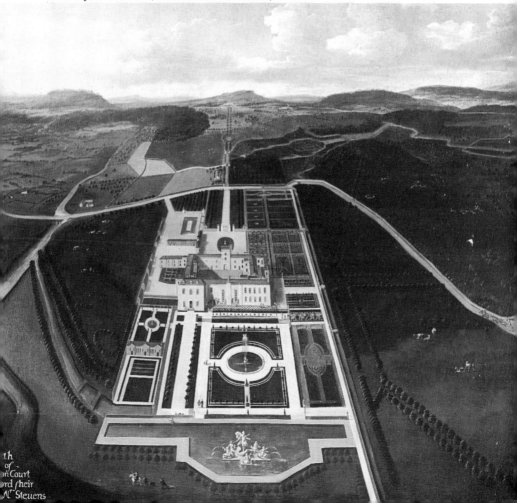

abundance those familiar Dutch features of clipped shrubs and numerous statues. At Dyrham, Avon, another follower of William III, William Blathwayt, had William Talman transform a rather less precipitous site with a vast layout of fountains, cascades and parterres. All these designs paled into insignificance when compared to the great garden laid out by London and Wise at Blenheim, Oxfordshire, the gift of a grateful sovereign to John Churchill, first Duke of Marlborough, a gift which subsequently was rather reluctantly paid for. Here London and Wise created an enormous parterre set within a hexagonal walled enclosure with bastioned corners almost as if they were fortifications designed to repel the French.

Contrasting with these great gardens were many much more modest ones to be found all over Britain. An excellent example which has been restored is that at Canons Ashby, Northamptonshire, which dates from between 1708 and 1717. Here there are a series of four walled gardens laid out to an axial design descending a gentle slope away from the south front of the house, the lowest one being a wilderness. This main vista was continued by a double elm avenue across the small park whilst on the west side of the house is a walled garden known as the Green Court with a lawn embellished with a formal arrangement of statues and clipped shrubs.

Then there were many quite small gardens attached to houses in towns. Few towns at this period were so large or so densely built up as to preclude virtually all the houses having at least small gardens. Most of these modest gardens have long since disappeared without trace but the plan of one such has survived on paper. This was the garden attached to the house in Nottingham where the defeated French Marshal Tallard spent his captivity in what would seem to be eminently civilised conditions. Although quite small, three rectangular gardens of varying size are fitted together at different levels, each with a parterre set out in grass, and with a little pavilion, or banqueting house, at the end of the garden in which the Marshal could sit to contemplate his affairs.

But perhaps the most enduring work done in the gardens of the period was the preparation of the perspective drawings of the great gardens of England by Leonard Knyff which were engraved by Joannes Kip. Knyff was another Dutchman, although he was in England some years before William became king, and his drawings have left us a magnificent record of the fine gardens of the period. They are not invariably an entirely accurate record since some, at least, of the plates were drawn to flatter the owners and convey an impression of immense grandeur, but from studies that have been made of surviving evidence on the ground most of the plates have proved to be quite accurate delineations.

Renaissance revived

During the eighteenth century the course of garden history was to undergo a fundamental change. From the concept of the garden as a place where the hand of man was imposed upon nature there developed the concept of the garden as an idealisation of nature. Now the objective of a garden was to be a piece of the natural landscape as it should, perhaps, have been created by the Almighty, but alas needed the mortal hand of the designer to emerge into its full beauty.

The creation of the landscape garden very largely eclipsed the traditional, formal gardens of the kind discussed in this book. In many cases this happened literally. An owner of a formal garden would decide to bring his garden up to date by calling upon the services of one of the professional landscape designers of the day. The fame of Lancelot Brown (1716-83), always known by his nickname of 'Capability' Brown, surpasses that of all his contemporaries but there were a number of such professional designers, many with a regional rather than a national fame. The new design would involve the creation of a great open park-like landscape with the sweeping grass sward reaching right up to the walls of the house. There was now no place for the rectangular, enclosed gardens of past centuries and all would be removed. Now flowers were banished to the walled kitchen garden along with the vegetables and other mundane things not fit to be seen from the windows of the house. The walled garden was itself usually sited some distance from the house.

The transformation was by no means universal. In southern England, and especially close to the capital, the change was very nearly complete, but further north, and especially in Scotland, there remained gardens of the old kind where the owners had either no inclination or lacked the means to undertake a transformation to the landscape garden style. Sometimes a house and garden became, by process of dynastic descent, a subsidiary house of the family. Perhaps it would become a dower house or become the residence of the agent of the estate. There would then be much less incentive to keep the garden up to date with the latest fashionable garden layout and the old garden would be left to slumber on along with the equally unfashionable house until, perhaps in the twentieth century, it would come to be appreciated once more, now as an interesting historical survival.

J. C. Loudon was among the first to show a real interest in the old gardens that had survived into the nineteenth century. His *Encyclopedia of Gardening* (1822) contains much historical information. On his frequent tours of Britain, looking at the great gardens of his day with a critical eye, he sometimes expressed approval for an old garden simply because the owner had resisted the temptation to change and had preserved intact a garden of the old type. Thus Knole, Wroxton, Busbridge and Bilston attracted his interest for here much of the old formal style of gardening had survived and was being preserved even though improvements had been made.

The development of a sense of history in gardens can be traced back to the eighteenth century. One of the complaints which Sir Uvedale Price (1747-1829) and Richard Payne Knight (1750-1824) put forward against the work of 'Capability' Brown and his fellow landscapers was that they heedlessly destroyed the earlier formal gardens which they found. But it was during the first decades of the nineteenth century that some sporadic efforts were made to restore and conserve the remaining formal gardens which had somehow survived. Avenues were felt to raise especially serious issues because partial preservation of an avenue makes little sense and it usually has to be all or nothing.

Avenues constitute such a dramatic feature that there were cases of avenues being preserved throughout the period when the naturalistic school of landscape parks held undisputed sway. Even Brown retained occasional avenues and lesser figures such as William Emes quite often seem to have incorporated the avenues of an earlier layout within the design of their landscape parks. Uvedale Price argued for the retention of avenues, even when they seemed to be wrongly sited, and the proponents of the picturesque in park and garden design generally favoured retaining avenues even though they argued against planting any new ones.

Loudon advocated the preservation of old gardens on the grounds that they constituted valuable evidence of the taste and practice of earlier generations. He was shocked by the intrusion of modern planting, such as the use of dahlias, in the topiary garden at Levens Hall, Cumbria. In this essentially historicist attitude he was well ahead of his time; indeed it was not until the latter decades of the nineteenth century that the remaining old gardens came to be generally regarded as precious survivals from an earlier time.

Even so there were quite a number of examples of attempts to create new gardens in what was supposed to be the old style of gardening. Humphry Repton designed an old English garden for Woburn Abbey, Bedfordshire, and a monastic garden for Ashridge, Hertfordshire, whilst William Pitt planted up a walled garden in what, he maintained, was a monastic style. Such gardens are to be seen in the light of the romantic fascination with 'olden times' which so pervaded the early years of the nineteenth century. They frequently seem to have been subordinate gardens within a larger layout, perhaps associated with a conservatory, an aviary or set within a walled garden.

It was some time before a formal design was felt to be appropriate to the immediate surroundings of the main house but by the 1830s the fashion for an area of formal design before the main façade of the house was well under way. Now the distant prospect of the landscape park laid out some half-century previously would be seen beyond the terrace garden with its surrounding balustrades and emblazoned with the elaborate planting made possible only by the latest horticultural techniques, such as bedding out. William Sawrey Gilpin (1762-1843) was among the most notable practitioners of this type of feature with his famous terraces at Clumber Park, Nottinghamshire, now alas gone. Sir Charles Barry (1795-1860), with his great terrace garden at Harewood House, West Yorkshire, was even more prolific.

Perhaps the most extraordinary garden to be created in this manner was that at Drummond Castle, Tayside. Here, Lewis Kennedy, assisted

Earlshall, Fife. Sir Robert Lorimer's design for the topiary garden suited to the tower house of the sixteenth century but not planted until the 1890s. (Drawing by H. Inigo Triggs.)

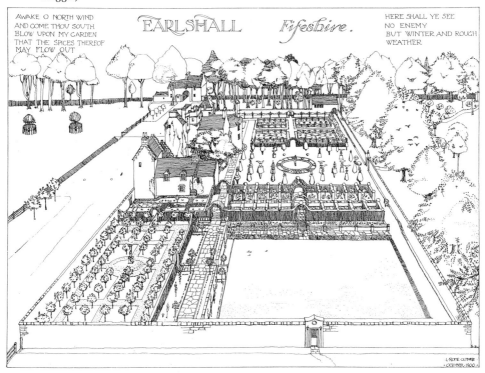

This parterre has been laid out amid the remains of Basing House, Hampshire, destroyed after being stormed by Oliver Cromwell in 1645.

by his son, George, recreated the garden known to have been there during the seventeenth century. During the 1820s and 1830s they rebuilt the terraces and laid out the vast parterre to a design based upon the saltire of Scotland. The planting paid little attention to historical evidence in that it incorporated such anachronisms as rhododendrons and heathers.

Such gardens, whilst vaguely felt by many to be evocative of the gardens of earlier times, soon came to be rejected by those of a more scholarly frame of mind who sought a return to the gardens which had been destroyed by the landscape garden school. Certainly by the 1880s the interest in the architecture and manners of 'olden times', which can perhaps be defined as the few centuries up to the seventeenth century, had progressed to the stage at which sincere efforts were being made to recreate the gardens of those centuries. The movement in architectural thought known as the Arts and Crafts movement was centred upon the traditional buildings of the Cotswolds. The garden which M. H. Baillie Scott laid out at Snowshill Manor, Gloucestershire, remains an excellent example and is now preserved by the National Trust. Such gardens were by no means restorations of anything known to have existed previously but new designs in what was understood to be the old style.

An important influence in the development of a more scholarly approach was the publication of Sir Reginald Blomfield's *The Formal Garden in England* in 1892. This is sometimes referred to as the earliest use of the word 'formal' in relation to gardens, but Sir Leslie Stephens had used the term in connection with the old style of pre-landscape gardens some years earlier in 1874.

This fascination with the old garden styles exerted a particularly strong influence upon owners of gardens which, for one reason or another, had never been kept up to date during the vogue for the landscape garden. At Melbourne Hall, Derbyshire, the formal garden laid out under the somewhat distant supervision of London and Wise in the early eighteenth century, and merely maintained during the decades when the house was a subsidiary residence of a family that had risen in the world, was recognised as a valuable historical survival and restored during the first decades of the twentieth century. Not far away the ninth Duke of Rutland began his life work of restoring his ancestral residence of Haddon Hall, Derbyshire, which had been uninhabited for more than a century after the Manners family had adopted Belvoir Castle as their main residence. During the 1920s the terraced gardens were returned to their original state and indeed acquired that romantic atmosphere which one suspects they can hardly have had when the work of the original garden designers was in its prime.

In Scotland the restorations carried out by Sir Robert Lorimer (1864-1929) as part of the restorations of old houses or castles are notable. Earlshall, Fife, was provided with a garden perhaps finer than anything that can have existed there when the house was lived in as a semi-fortified castle but the whole has that appropriateness which Lorimer was somehow able to bring to all his projects. His own garden at Kellie Castle, Fife, is a less elaborate garden of the same kind.

A characteristic of virtually all these reconstructions or restorations of formal gardens was that the planting was excluded from the historical features of the design. As long as the layout and the built features such as paths, walls and steps followed historical precedent the planting could be quite modern in character. This is true even of such otherwise admirable restoration works as that at Pitmedden, Grampian. It has been left to very recent times indeed for the planting to be designed on an historical basis comparable to that adopted for the layout and construction.

Further reading

Blomfield, Sir Reginald. *The Formal Garden in England*. Macmillan, 1892.

Green, David. *Gardener to Queen Anne, Henry Wise and the Formal Garden*. Oxford University Press, 1956.

Hadfield, Miles. *A History of British Gardening*. Spring Books, 1969; John Murray, 1979. Originally published as *Gardening in Britain*, Hutchinson, 1960.

Hunt, John Dixon. *Garden and Grove*. Dent, 1986.

Jacques, David, and Horst, Arend van der. *The Gardens of William and Mary*. Christopher Helm, 1988.

Little, G. Allan (editor). *Scotland's Gardens*. Spurbooks, 1981.

Strong, Roy. *The Renaissance Garden in England*. Thames and Hudson, 1979.

Thacker, Christopher. *The History of Gardens*. Croom Helm, 1979.

Triggs, H. Inigo. *Formal Gardens in England and Scotland*. Batsford, 1902.

Gardens to visit

There are few Renaissance gardens in Britain which are preserved in anything approaching their original condition. Because of the need to renew the living materials of which gardens are largely composed, all have been replanted during subsequent centuries. In some gardens, however, one can still obtain a vivid idea of what it must have been like to walk in a garden of the sixteenth to eighteenth centuries. Some of the best gardens for this purpose are completely new constructions.

The following is a select list of gardens in Britain which are worth visiting as examples of Renaissance gardens. Before making a special journey intending visitors are advised to confirm dates and times of opening by telephone or by reference to *Historic Houses, Castles and Gardens Open to the Public in Great Britain and Ireland* (British Leisure Publications, Windsor Court, East Grinstead, West Sussex RH19 1XA), obtainable at most booksellers.

Albury Park, Albury, Guildford, Surrey. Telephone: 048641 2964.
The gardens were laid out by John and George Evelyn from 1655 with terraces to the north of the house. Beneath the main terrace is a cavern dated 1676.

Blickling Hall, Blickling, Aylsham, Norfolk NR11 6NF (National Trust). Telephone: 0263 733084.

The large formal garden to the east of the house remains from the early layout of the gardens, along with parts of a wilderness. It was much extended and replanted later.

Bramham Park, Wetherby, West Yorkshire LS23 6ND. Telephone: 0937 844265.

This early eighteenth-century woodland garden has radiating *allées* in the French manner.

Canons Ashby House, Canons Ashby, Daventry, Northamptonshire NN11 6SD (National Trust). Telephone: 0327 860044.

There are formal gardens with terraces, and gatepiers of 1710.

Chastleton House (Oxfordshire), near Moreton-in-Marsh, Gloucestershire. Telephone: 060874 355.

Two topiary gardens remain of the garden layout of *c*.1700.

Chatsworth, Bakewell, Derbyshire DE4 1PP. Telephone: 0246 582204.

Features of the late seventeenth-, early eighteenth-century gardens remain including the great cascade, pools and fountains, now set within a later landscape park.

Edzell Castle, Edzell, Tayside. Telephone: 031-244 3101.

This tower house has an early seventeenth-century pleasance — a garden enclosed by elaborately sculptured walls.

Erddig, Wrexham, Clwyd LL13 0YT (National Trust). Telephone: 0978 355314.

This is an impressive example of a garden of the early eighteenth century, just prior to the vogue for landscape gardens. It has been extensively restored and replanted by the National Trust.

Greenwich Park, London SE10.

This is a Royal Park long open to the public. Traces of the former grandeur of the seventeenth-century layout can still be detected in spite of current neglect.

Haddon Hall, Bakewell, Derbyshire DE4 1LA. Telephone: 0629 812855.

The seventeenth-century gardens form a series of terraces on the south side of the house. They were carefully restored in the early twentieth century.

Ham House, Ham, Richmond, Surrey TW10 7RS. Telephone: 081-940 1950.

The grounds are of 1671-93 with lawns intersected by gravel walks, a wilderness and small gardens enclosed by covered *allées*. They have been much restored and replanted by the National Trust.

Hampton Court Palace (Middlesex), East Molesey, Surrey KT8 9AH. Telephone: 081-977 8441.

Much remains of the magnificent gardens laid out here for successive monarchs. The Pond and Privy Gardens are to the south of the palace whilst to the east lies the Fountain Garden with the Long Water as the centrepiece to the great prospect across the park eastwards. The well known maze is a much replanted part of the Wilderness to the north of the palace.

Hardwick Hall, Doe Lea, Chesterfield, Derbyshire S44 5QJ (National Trust). Telephone: 0246 850430.

The original garden layout survives around this early seventeenth-century 'prodigy' house. There are elaborately crested garden walls.

Hatfield House, Hatfield, Hertfordshire AL9 5NF. Telephone: 0707 262823.

The gardens here have been developed over a long period but always with a generally seventeenth-century appearance.

Kew Palace, Royal Botanic Gardens, Kew, Richmond, Surrey. Telephone: 081-940 3321.

Between the Thames and the palace is the Queen's Garden, a garden in the style of about 1630 which was laid out in 1969.

Kirby Hall, Deene, near Corby, Northamptonshire NN17 3EN (English Heritage). Telephone: 0536 203230.

Substantial works are in progress to restore the west garden of this Elizabethan mansion.

Levens Hall, Levens, Kendal, Cumbria LA8 0PB. Telephone: 05395 60321.

The famous topiary garden was originally planted between 1689 and 1712 but much replanted and extended in the early nineteenth century.

Little Moreton Hall, Congleton, Cheshire (National Trust). Telephone: 0260 272018.

A recently planted knot garden is based on a plan of 1680. As no records of the original gardens survive this is a new garden in an old style.

Melbourne Hall, Melbourne, Derby DE7 1EN. Telephone: 0332 862502.
The late seventeenth-, early eighteenth-century formal garden was laid out under the direction of London and Wise. The woodland garden with *allées* is in the style of Le Nôtre.

Montacute House, Montacute, Yeovil, Somerset TA15 6XP (National Trust). Telephone: 0935 823289.
The design of the formal gardens has survived largely intact although they were much reconstructed in the late nineteenth century.

Moseley Old Hall (Staffordshire), near Wolverhampton, West Midlands (National Trust). Telephone: 0902 782808.
This recreated garden is based on a plan of the 1630s. The parterre of box and gravel is planted with trees.

Museum of Garden History, St Mary-at-Lambeth, Lambeth Palace Road, London SE1. Telephone: 071-373 4030.
In the churchyard of the former church of St Mary-at-Lambeth, by the gate of Lambeth Palace, a garden of generally mid seventeenth-century type has been laid out.

Oxford Botanic Garden, High Street, Oxford. Telephone: 0865 276920.
The oldest botanic garden in Britain was founded here in 1621. It retains the atmosphere of a physic garden with its original gates and walls and orderly beds of plants.

Packwood House (Warwickshire), Lapworth, Solihull, West Midlands B94 6AT (National Trust). Telephone: 05643 2024.
This mid seventeenth-century formal garden includes a yew garden said to represent the Sermon on the Mount.

Pitmedden Garden, Ellon, Aberdeenshire AB4 0BD (National Trust for Scotland). Telephone: 06513 2352.
The gardens, originally laid out in 1664-75, have been restored by the National Trust for Scotland to a design derived from those shown in a view of Holyroodhouse, Edinburgh, of 1647.

Powis Castle, Welshpool, Powys SY21 8RF (National Trust). Telephone: 0938 4336.
The fine terraced gardens are probably of early eighteenth-century origin.

Red Lodge, Park Row, Bristol, Avon BS1 5LJ. Telephone: 0272 299771.
There is a recently constructed rectangular knot garden to the rear of this museum. It is on a site known to have been a garden but of which no records survive.

St Paul's Walden Bury, Whitwell, near Hitchin, Hertfordshire. Telephone: 043887 218 or 219.
The early eighteenth-century park was laid out under the strong influence of the school of Le Nôtre.

Tudor House Museum, Bugle Street, Southampton, Hampshire. Telephone: 0703 224216.
A garden of early seventeenth-century style has been laid out adjoining the museum as one of the exhibits.

Westbury Court, Westbury-on-Severn, Gloucestershire GL14 1PD (National Trust). Telephone: 045276 461.
The formal water garden of 1694-1705 has been restored by the National Trust.

Powis Castle, Powys: the yew arbour from which to view the impressive terraces.

Index

Page numbers in italic refer to illustrations.